Praise for
No More Dreaded Mondays

"Authentic work involves much more than just getting a paycheck. In *No More Dreaded Mondays*, Dan Miller captures the soul of work—how each of us can take our unique, God-given talents and blend those into meaningful, purposeful, and profitable work."

—DAVE RAMSEY, host of *The Dave Ramsey Show* and author of *The Total Money Makeover*

"As every millionaire knows, you'll never gain wealth and financial security by working in a job you hate. *No More Dreaded Mondays* provides an inspiring road map on how to find meaningful work and financial freedom."

—T. HARV EKER, author of the national bestseller *Secrets of the Millionaire Mind*

"With this inspiring book, Dan Miller shows how to make Monday the first day of the rest of your life."

—DANIEL H. PINK, author of *A Whole New Mind*

"Dan Miller inspires his readers to a higher calling in their work. With opportunities all around us, no one should be content with simply creating income. Meaningful work is part of living out God's purpose in our lives. *No More Dreaded Mondays* shows you the way to find your unique application."

—ZIG ZIGLAR, best-selling author of *See You at the Top*

No More Dreaded Mondays

Ignite Your Passion—And Other Revolutionary Ways
to Discover Your True Calling at Work

Dan Miller

WATERBROOK
PRESS

NO MORE DREADED MONDAYS
PUBLISHED BY WATERBROOK PRESS
12265 Oracle Boulevard, Suite 200
Colorado Springs, Colorado 80921

All Scripture quotations, unless otherwise indicated, are taken from the King James
Version. Scripture quotations marked (NIV) are taken from the Holy Bible, New
International Version®. NIV®. Copyright © 1973, 1978, 1984 by International
Bible Society. Used by permission of Zondervan Publishing House. All rights reserved.
Scripture quotations marked (GNT) are taken from the Good News Translation—Second
Edition. Copyright © 1992 by American Bible Society. Used by permission. Scripture
quotations marked (TLB) are taken from The Living Bible, copyright © 1971. Used
by permission of Tyndale House Publishers Inc., Wheaton, Illinois 60189. All rights
reserved. Scripture quotations marked (CEV) are taken from the Contemporary
English Version. Copyright © 1991, 1992, 1995 by American Bible Society. Used by
permission. Scripture quotations marked (HCSB) are taken from The Holman Christian
Standard Bible®, © copyright 1999, 2000, 2002, 2003 by Holman Bible Publishers.
Used by permission.

Italicized words in Scripture quotations reflect the author's emphasis.

ISBN: 978-1-4000-7385-6

Published in association with Yates & Yates, Orange, California.

Published in the United States by WaterBrook Multnomah, an imprint of the Crown
Publishing Group, a division of Random House Inc., New York.

WATERBROOK and its deer design logo are registered trademarks of WaterBrook Press,
a division of Random House Inc.

This book is copublished with Broadway Business, an imprint of the Crown Publishing
Group, a division of Random House Inc., New York.

Cataloging-in-Publication Data is on file with the Library of Congress.

Printed in the United States of America
2011

10 9 8 7 6 5 4 3 2

SPECIAL SALES
WaterBrook Press books are available at special discounts for bulk purchases for sales
promotions or premiums. Special editions, including personalized covers, excerpts of
existing books, and corporate imprints, can be created in large quantities for special
needs. For more information, write to Special Markets, WaterBrook Press,
specialmarkets@randomhouse.com.

To my dad, Ray F Miller, who taught me that work was not something to be avoided, but rather something to be done with wholehearted effort, character, and integrity. Your model of believing we are temporary stewards of animals, tools, land, and friendships continues to call me to a daily accountability of those resources.

CONTENTS

ACKNOWLEDGMENTS

I want to thank the crowd of mentors who began shaping my thinking and expanding my expectations years ago on that dairy farm in Ohio. With no TV in our home, I discovered the amazing world of books as a child. Those opened the door to the unusual and creative life I am privileged to live today. People such as Earl Nightingale, Norman Vincent Peale, Robert Schuller, Mark Victor Hansen, Denis Waitley, and Brian Tracy served as my mentors and guides through the powerful means of the written word. Zig Ziglar's powerful personal presentations captivated me many years ago and called me to a higher level of success without compromising integrity or compassion.

I thank my wife, Joanne, who has been the main supporting character in my life story for more than forty years. My days begin and end with your unwavering support and prayers. Your enthusiasm for my unusual projects has allowed me to explore unknown territory and achieve a kind of success envied by any person in the world. To my incredible children, Kevin, Jared, and Ashley, I offer thanks for participating in the ups and downs of a dad who could not settle for common work. And now as adults each of you continues to make valuable contributions to my work as you discover your own unique calling.

Thanks to my Wednesday morning Eagles group. You eleven guys truly provide the format for "iron sharpening iron." The wit, wisdom, and unvarnished feedback from this amazing group of writers and deep thinkers have helped my growth, both personally and as a writer.

Thanks to my agent Curtis Yates and the entire team at Yates & Yates for stretching me beyond my own vision for this project. Your honesty, persistence, and stress-relieving humor proved to be valuable constants in the process of bringing *No More Dreaded Mondays* to life.

Thanks to Michael Palgon at Random House for immediately "getting" this message and for championing it to the team you assembled. Thanks to Sarah Rainone for your expertise in polishing every page of this work, adding clarity and a flow to my assortment of stories and concepts. My gratitude goes to Ron Lee at WaterBrook for your thoughtful additions for making this a relevant and spiritually inspiring work. To Meredith McGinnis, Elizabeth Hazelton, Roger Scholl, and Joel Kneedler, thanks for your excitement and contributions for positioning and marketing this book.

Finally, I want to thank you, loyal readers and clients, who so willingly have shared your life stories through the years. Your exhilarating and sometimes terrifying transitions into fulfilling and meaningful work are the foundation for the *No More Dreaded Mondays* principles. As pioneers and trailblazers you have prepared the path for the many who will see new possibilities and live richer lives as a result.

INTRODUCTION

Have you ever said "Thank God it's Monday"? Why is that such an unbelievable statement? Why does "Thank God it's *Friday*" just roll off your tongue? Why is TGIF an instantly recognizable acronym for the relief we feel at the end of a workweek, knowing we can spend the weekend doing something enjoyable? Why do we thank God for saving us from the one thing in which we invest up to 50 percent of our waking hours? If we dread the work we are doing, is it an honorable use of our time? Do you really think it's possible to fulfill your purpose if you're doing work that is not meaningful and fulfilling?

Maybe you're one of the many who have gotten caught up in thinking work is just something you do to support your weekends. Work is that necessary evil in our lives, a means to an end, or just a curse from God. You probably take your role of providing for yourself and those depending on you seriously. But you don't expect to enjoy your work—you just do what has to be done.

Only now you're seeing that even loyalty and dependability bring no guarantees. Lately you've seen coworkers who have been let go after years of faithful service. Perhaps your entire industry has been shaken by outsourcing or changing technology. Maybe you're tired of the long commute and being tied to your desk when you know you could make your own hours and still be productive. You may have ideas stirring that you think could create new income and time freedom.

But here comes another Monday. Maybe feeling trapped is just the reality of the way things are. Doesn't everyone dread Mondays? Don't we put our true *calling* on the shelf when we leave for work on Monday morning? Does our work even matter in the final evaluation of a life well lived? Don't all responsible people just bury their dreams and passions in exchange for getting a paycheck?

Absolutely not! Let me assure you that it doesn't need to be this way at all. All of us, no matter how old we are or what kind of work we're doing, can learn to bring the same excitement to our jobs that we bring to whatever we love to do on our days off. I believe that each one of us can pursue work that is a reflection of our best selves—a true fulfillment of our callings. What we do on Mondays is a more visible expression of our applied faith than how we spend fifty-eight minutes on Sunday morning.

For many of you, *No More Dreaded Mondays* will present a process of waking up the dreams and passions you had as a child. Have you ever met an unimaginative five year old? Probably not. When you were five, you probably had a dream. Maybe in the still of the night you thought you heard God speaking to you—calling you to a certain type of life and a special kind of work.

So what happened? Well, life happened. Along the way, in our desire to be responsible, practical, and realistic adults, too many of us wildly imaginative kids lost touch with our creative abilities and gave up a commitment to translating our dreams into enjoyable and fulfilling work. But it doesn't need to be that way. All of us, no matter how old we are or what kind of work we're doing, can learn to bring that authentic, childlike creativity to our work.

In fact, the moment you express a desire for something more than repetitive, meaningless work, something more than simply punching the clock, the moment you realize that meaningful, purposeful, and profitable work really *is* a possibility, you've already taken an important step toward reawakening the dreams and passions you haven't had in years—or might never have had at all. All of a sudden, complacency and "comfortable misery" become intolerable. The idea of putting your *calling* on the shelf becomes intolerable. Not only do we have the opportunity, we have the *responsibility* to spend our working hours in work that will elevate us to our highest calling and transform the world around us.

No More Dreaded Mondays will show you that meaningful work really is within your grasp. It will help you recapture that childlike creativity you may have lost. It may release the dreams and sense of purpose you had as a child. You may find your prayers invigorated, now knowing there is a day-by-day application of God's design for your life. And once you've opened the door and seen all the exciting career opportunities that await you— whether you decide to revolutionize your current job or launch a new career altogether—you'll find you can't go back to the old way of working. It's like you've fanned to life some dying embers, ignited a new flame of possibility. That inner light of your childhood imagination might have been dimmed by your "adult" notions of work, but this book will help you rekindle it again so that you get a real sense of all the possibilities available to you.

We can find ways to express our hopes and dreams in our daily work. While I certainly don't advocate confusing "who we are" with "what we do," I believe that our work can be our best gift to ourselves, our friends and family, our communities—and the best expression of our purpose here on earth. Given the amount of time we spend working, failure to find meaningful, significant work is not just a minor misstep in living out God's plan; it is a deeper kind of failure that can make each day feel like living death.

It's no surprise that we often choose to dismiss work's importance by reducing it to a necessary evil that merely provides a paycheck. But as long as we view work as simply something we have to do to pay the bills, we keep ourselves from embracing our talents and gifts, from recognizing our visions, dreams, and passions. Fulfilling work, work that integrates our talents and our passions, work done for a worthy purpose, has always been a sign of inner—and outer—maturity and wisdom.

And there's an even more urgent need to seek out more meaningful work. In today's fast-changing world, we can no longer afford to simply show up at work, punch a clock, and expect payment for our time; in fact, we put ourselves at tremendous risk if we do. Many of us have been raised to think that all we need to do to achieve success and security is finish school, get a job with the right company, put in 35 years or so, and wait for the proverbial gold watch. But those days are over, never to return. In today's volatile workplace, the average job lasts a mere 3.2 years. Companies are dismantling pension plans, cutting health insurance benefits, and replacing the gold watch with a pink slip. So has the workplace become a hostile environment? Have all the good opportunities disappeared? Have we been doomed to lives of financial mediocrity and soul-crushing work conditions? The answer to each of these questions is a resounding no.

But the workplace *has* changed. And we need to change along with it. We need to change the way we think about our jobs, about work hours and salaries, and about job security. As we witness the destruction of the old model of work, is it possible to imagine a new model that's about more than drudgery, boredom, and a paycheck that's never enough? The answer is an enthusiastic yes. Everywhere you look, you'll find new and exciting opportunities. Keep in mind, however, they are a lot different from the choices of previous generations.

I have had the privilege of experiencing these changes firsthand, so I know how scary and intimidating they may seem at first. The future that was presented to me when I was a young boy was a lot different from the varied but exciting path I have taken. If I had followed the career path my parents laid out for me, there's a strong possibility that today I'd dread Mondays and despise my daily work as many of you do. Breaking away from the life expected of me was not easy; in fact, it caused a severe breach in my relationship with my parents, as walking away from the work also meant leaving my family's religious culture. But I'm forever grateful that I did not forsake my search for my true calling—for a daily enriching spiritual life and work that fulfills God's purpose for my life. And let me add that time is a wonderful healer. As with any change, there are fears and growing pains associated with the search for meaningful work. Over time, however, I was able to reestablish family bonds and share the joys not only of connecting grandparents with grandchildren but also of newly discovered meaningful work.

I was born into a conservative rural Ohio family. Torn between the need to provide for our family and the desire to embrace his spiritual calling, my father both worked as a farmer and served as pastor to the little local Mennonite church. His double life instilled in me the idea that work was just a necessary evil, while a *calling* had to be squeezed in around the realistic demands of working. Hard work meant being responsible, and it left little time for anything playful or pleasurable. Frankly, anything that provided enjoyment was suspected as being self-serving, which further reinforced the idea that there was no merit in expecting joy in work. Amusement parks, fancy cars, TV viewing, ball games, and higher education were more examples of useless and dangerous activities that would likely pull a person away from what was eternally important. Exhausting farmwork was a matter of survival; *work that you enjoyed demonstrated egotistical selfishness.*

Despite the limitations on the things I could do or the places I could go, nothing could stop my mind from wandering. As I was working out in the fields, I was also imagining a world I had never seen.

Somehow in that restricted world, when I was about twelve years old, I was able to get a copy of the little 33⅓ rpm record by Earl Nightingale titled *The Strangest Secret.* On it I heard this gravelly-voiced man say that I could be everything I wanted to be by simply changing my thinking. He talked about six words that could dramatically affect the results of my best efforts: *We become what we think about.* I recognized that, if that were true, the possibilities of what I could do with my life were limitless. Nightingale's Secret, the Biblical principle "As a man thinketh in his heart, so is he," and Norman Vincent Peale's *Power of Positive Thinking* all came alive as more than just words.

Knowing this radical way of thinking would not be welcome in my house, I hid that little record under my mattress, bringing it out night after night to hear again the promises of a better life. While friends were hiding their girlie magazines under their beds, it was this message of hope and opportunity that captured my imagination.

I began to see the impact of that thinking on my belief system. Any complacency I might have held about my future disappeared forever. I became intensely curious about the world and began to explore the way things worked, how they could be made better, and what possibilities existed for change and innovation. I would take the lawn mower engine apart to see if I could improve its power and efficiency. I improvised new machines and inventions from old parts I salvaged from the local dump. I was drawn to the Biblical stories of Joshua, Joseph, and Solomon. I saw them as examples of people who dreamed things that others thought impossible and who created plans of action to make their dreams a reality.

I became adept at coming up with new solutions to problems in my little world. Since we lived miles out in the country and it was impossible to get to town on my own to see my buddies, I devised a way to turn our small Ford tractor into a makeshift hot rod. I took the rear-end assembly from a junk car and attached the driveshaft to the power takeoff (PTO) on the tractor. After pushing the tractor to maximum speed, I could take it out of gear, engage the PTO, and push the tractor much faster than it was ever intended to go.

The farming environment exposed me to carpentry, plumbing, and electrical and mechanical systems, but I began to seek out new opportunities—everything from selling Christmas cards to setting up my first roadside business—wherever I could. After my mother canned all the sweet corn our cellars would hold, I would get up at five o'clock in the morning, go out and pick the remaining corn, and head for the main road with our little tractor and a trailer full of excess corn. With my homemade sign, I would sell ears of corn for thirty cents a dozen and collect my growing nest egg. Meanwhile, my infatuation with fast and fancy cars grew stronger, thanks in part to the fact that my grandparents on both sides were horse-and-buggy Amish—no cars were allowed in their households. Even when my parents decided they would have a car, the car had to be black. Some of you have undoubtedly experienced the attraction of those things that are forbidden by religious legalism.

My first car was entirely handmade. When I was eighteen years old, I purchased a 1931 Model A Ford for fifty dollars. Slowly and meticulously, I began building a running street rod. Every time I found myself with an extra five dollars, instead of blowing it on candy or clothes, I would go to the junkyard and buy a generator or a set of seats. I learned by doing, as well as by listening and talking to anyone who knew more than I did. Remember, I didn't have a dad who would take me into town to purchase a "cool" car. In our family, cars were strictly for transportation. Anything that accented visual appeal or high performance was nothing but "worldly." So while my friends conned their parents into buying them their first cars, I put in every spare minute in that unheated old chicken coop where I was building my car. One year later I drove out with an eye-stopping hot rod with a Chrysler hemi engine. This simple farm kid suddenly had a car that outshone those of most of my friends.

Seeing these simple dreams come true fueled my desire for new experiences. Upon completing high school, I was expected to become a full-time member of our family farming operation. But I wanted more, and I knew that college would help open new doors for me. Against my father's wishes, I decided to further my education. I was required to help with the dairy and farming chores beginning at 5:30 A.M. But I didn't let that little detail deter me. I enrolled in a branch campus of Ohio State University, where I could attend classes from 6:00 to 10:00 P.M.

As a poor kid with good grades, I qualified for an eighteen-hundred-dollar tuition grant. However, my predilection for seeing things in new ways was already hindering a "normal" view of having money in the bank. The tuition was not payable immediately but would be due over the next several months—which meant I had eighteen hundred dollars in hard, cold cash sitting in my bank account.

Surely, I thought, I could leverage that money into something more. I responded to an ad in a magazine much like the ones many of you have seen: "Get into the vending business; you don't have to sell anything. We install the machines—all you have to do is collect the money." My eighteen hundred dollars purchased ten hot cashew machines. *What could be more appealing than hot cashews?* I thought. Cashews are the perfect snack food—wholesome, nutritious, and a perfect complement to any beverage. This was going to be too easy. I envisioned my machines finding homes in ballparks, family recreation centers, and the local convenience store. But things didn't turn out exactly as I had planned.

A representative came to place the machines. Unfortunately, the company rep preferred to locate the machines in the sleaziest bars he could find. Picture it: a shy, backward Mennonite kid discovering that his machines were being installed in places he himself had never been allowed to enter.

Guess what else didn't turn out as I expected. Do you know what happens to cashews under heat if they are not stirred about once every twelve hours? They *mold*! I immediately began getting calls from these sordid establishments telling me to get those machines out or suffer the wrath of their inebriated customers. I picked up my ten precious machines and hid them in an old storage shed where my dad would never be made aware of my stupidity. Months later I sold them for roughly ten cents on the dollar. When it came time to pay my tuition, I had to get out and hustle for the money I had lost. I squeezed in odd jobs around my already busy schedule of farm chores and college classes. It was my first of many painful lessons that looking for a quick buck is typically a recipe for disaster.

The key to real success is not about jumping on the latest, greatest idea you read about in a magazine or on some website; it's not about trying to make a quick buck. It's about knowing yourself so completely that you can identify a work fit that you will find enjoyable, rewarding, and profitable. Unfortunately, I was a slow learner. This was not the last time I found myself on the receiving end of this message. Years later, I was reminded of this basic principle again after buying a health and fitness center. Now keep in mind, I personally don't like the fitness center environment. I am much too impatient for the socializing and the slow pace of workouts in that setting. But I saw the bottom line and thought I could make money. Boy, was I wrong. After three frustrating years, I sold that business at public auction, taking about a $430,000 loss. It was just another of the many hard lessons that taught me the importance of finding a proper fit when it comes to type of work and work model.

Now, the answer was not to take the safe path and avoid taking chances, but rather to stay true to my unique, God-given talents and not try to duplicate the successes of someone else. This is one of the core concepts of *No More Dreaded Mondays:* You have to look inward for the keys to your success. Knowing yourself well will give you the necessary insight for choosing work that leads to both fulfillment and financial rewards. Trying to mimic someone else's success will usually lead to heartache and disappointment.

Since the fitness center disaster, I've been a lot more honest with myself about the kind of work that's right for me. I have built service businesses and provided consulting, speaking, and public seminars. Along the way I got multiple college degrees in my ever-expanding quest for new knowledge and information. I even found time to marry a beautiful wife and be a daddy to three wonderful children. For decades my wife has loved me, encouraged me, and helped me through all of this learning, mistake making, and learning all over again. Today I provide executive career coaching, develop innovative personal improvement products, write books, and run a virtual business. While my businesses have neither physical facilities nor employees, I have multiple revenue streams and an income that puts me in the top 3 percent of America's earners. My family's lives are streamlined and focused. My wife and I have more control of our time than we had imagined was possible. Our children and grandchildren are integral parts of our work and play activities. We enjoy the feedback of other people who have benefited from our efforts and consider ourselves to be truly blessed with the multiple characteristics of true success.

Let me emphasize that the process of getting here was not wasted time. I loved the variety of things I did—and I don't regret the bad choices. I was not prepared or qualified by life experiences at twenty-five or thirty-five to do what I do today. There is value in the process of finding your true calling—and it may include some bumps along the way. I know we all wish for that "road to Damascus" experience where God clearly and dramatically reveals the plan for our life. But in my experience, clarity doesn't often come in that way.

If you are always successful, it's unlikely that you've really stretched yourself to see what you are capable of doing. Like a high jumper, if you always clear the bar, you don't really know how good you could be. It's only when you trip the bar that you have a true indication of where your limits lie. Don't be afraid of failing, for it's in failing that we grow and expand our boundaries. A life of seeking God's perfect will and path does not guarantee a smooth and trouble-free journey. "If you wait until the wind and the weather are just right, you will never plant anything and never harvest anything" (Ecclesiastes 11:4, GNT).

It is out of this backdrop that the material in *No More Dreaded Mondays* has been refined. I hope you can bypass some of the lessons I learned from the school of hard knocks and still experience the absolute joy that I have had in finding meaningful and fulfilling work. Even on Monday mornings.

No More Dreaded Mondays will walk you through the process of embracing change—even when that change is unexpected and unwelcome. We'll see how old models of work are disappearing but new ones are unfolding right before our eyes. We'll explore how to recognize and capitalize on these changes. You won't have the job your mom or dad did, but you can prosper and thrive as you put yourself in the driver's seat of your work life. You can identify your best fit as an employee, a free agent, an independent contractor, a contingency worker, a consultant, an entrepreneur, or a business owner and be confident that you have chosen meaningful, fulfilling work. The Bible doesn't talk about computer programming or being an airline pilot, but it gives us solid principles for work that matters. Your options are not shrinking, they are expanding. You've shattered any comfortable misery. You're past the point of ever being content with just getting a paycheck. Get ready to remove forever the stigma of Monday mornings. From now on, every day is Friday!

1

DON'T BE "STUPID"

William and his wife, Bonnie, were smiling when they walked into my office, but it was clear they had a lot on their minds. They were worried about their financial future and eager for advice. Both were attractive, vibrant professionals who were clearly confident and successful. At fifty-three years old, William had been a commercial pilot with a major airline for twenty-seven years. His annual salary was more than $200,000, and years earlier he had calculated that, with his investments and his pension, he could retire in high style by age fifty-six. But then his investments took a big dive and the airline defaulted on its pension plan. Suddenly it seemed uncertain that he'd even have a job for three more years, let alone the money to stop working.

William and Bonnie are not alone in having their career path and financial plans disappear within months. The status of most employee pension plans sits somewhere between threatened and dead and gone. IBM has announced it will discontinue pension benefits starting in 2008 and shift to 401(k) plans that will save the company as much as $3 billion over the next few years. Following the lead of United and US Airways, other major airlines have proposed dumping their pensions in bankruptcy. Allstate Insurance has "invited" all 6,200 of its agents to become independent contractors, giving up their health insurance and pension benefits in the process. There is no way the federal Pension Benefit Guaranty Corporation can back up these folding pension plans. The PBGC is already on the hook for $62.3 billion in expected pension payouts with only $390 billion in its accounts. So where does this leave you and me?

"Revolutionary" Thinking

As I told William and Bonnie, if you think like a traditional "employee," you are placing yourself in jeopardy. We are witnessing the dawn of a revolution in which each one of us will become completely responsible for our own income, benefits, and retirement. But don't assume this is a negative transition—in fact, what I'm going to reveal in these pages is that never before have we had so many opportunities to take control over the shape of our careers. Never before has the potential for fulfilling work and true wealth been greater. Sure, the times, they are a-changing. But you can stay ahead of the inevitable changes—and benefit from them—by *seeing* the wealth of new opportunities available to you and planning for them now.

While my use of the word *Revolutionary* may conjure up the idea of donning a pointy hat and bringing a cannon in to work tomorrow, that's not exactly what I have in mind. The dictionary defines *revolutionary* as "radically new or innovative; outside or beyond established procedure, principles, etc.," as in a revolutionary discovery. It's revolutionary to become more than simply complacent in your workplace. After all, the traditional employee does not often embrace radically new or innovative thinking—and frequently does not think much at all. The traditional employee does what he or she is expected to do, completes established procedures, and makes sure things are done today the same way they were done yesterday. Revolutionaries pave their own ways; they stretch the rules and think of ways to do things *better*. A brief warning: Revolutionaries may be seen as threats to the status quo. I even have a close friend who was fired for "thinking too much." In traditional work positions, the requirements of the job are frequently imposed on you, regardless of your passions, calling, or unique skills. But what kind of way is this to spend the majority of your waking life? Wasn't my friend's firing really a kind of liberation?

And what about you? Does your work really allow you to make the best use of your abilities, your personality traits, your values and dreams? If you were to pull the paycheck blindfold off your eyes, would you see work that's authentically fulfilling?

If you are committed to a life of purpose and meaning, your work will necessarily become something more than a tool to make money. Work itself will become a sacred experience, a channel through which you shine your unique light, extend your love, and make a difference in the world. We can transform our work by seeing it as the primary application of our purpose rather than a necessary and practical evil. We will shift from viewing work as something that serves only our own needs to seeing it as a calling that enables us to serve others, share God's love, and activate a chain of miracles. "Anyone, then, who knows the good he ought to do and doesn't do it, sins" (James 4:17, NIV).

Have You Made the Most of the Life You Have?

- Are you where you thought you'd be at this stage of your life?
- Have you ever had a sense of God's calling?
- How did you hear that calling?
- Is your work a fulfillment of your calling?
- Do you go home at night with a sense of meaning, purpose, and accomplishment?
- If nothing changed in your life over the next five years, would that be okay?
- If you want different results next year, what are you willing to change about what you are doing now?

Within the pages of *No More Dreaded Mondays*, you will discover new opportunities and rediscover things about yourself that will provide you with a sense of meaning, accomplishment, and fulfillment. This book is filled with practical advice on how to move from traditional work to an authentic—and perhaps revolutionary—investment of your time and energy. And as you become a Revolutionary, you will find the preceding questions much easier to answer.

> *Success is never an accident. It typically starts as imagination, becomes a dream, stimulates a goal, grows into a plan of action—which then inevitably meets with opportunity. Don't get stuck along the way.*

Sit Straight and Stay in the Lines . . . Why?

Unfortunately, from the first day of school, our academic system has been teaching us to work in a workplace that is disappearing. We were told to sit up straight, talk only when it was our turn, walk in an orderly fashion to the lunchroom, follow instructions, and color inside the lines. These instructions encourage the mind-set we can refer to as "paycheck mentality." As children, we learn that, if we go by the rules, do what we're told, we will be rewarded. Do what the teacher says, and you'll get good grades. Naturally these lessons prepare us for a paycheck mentality: Show up for work, don't make waves, and put in your time. With these skills you can get a paycheck, but you probably won't be equipped for the revolution in the workplace that will liberate you from the old way of working: mind-numbing and often poorly paid production- and knowledge-based work models. By *production work* I mean the repetitive work done in factories and on assembly lines. By *knowledge work* I mean the kind that involves managing data and analyzing information. Not only are these models outdated and soul-stripping, but they're endangered by technology and easily outsourced. *Revolutionaries,* by contrast, may change what they do every day; they look for results, they *don't* watch for how many hours they have worked, and they work in ways that may be unique and surprising.

He who rejects change is the architect of decay. The only human institution which rejects progress is the cemetery.
　　　　　　　　　　　　—Harold Wilson

According to the late Peter Drucker, we are reaching the end of a forty-year period (1970–2010) that has brought more change than the world has ever seen—and there's more where that came from. As we approach the end of this time frame, the speed of change is increasing. The U.S. Bureau of Labor Statistics is now predicting that 50 percent of the jobs we will have in the next ten years have not yet been created. Bureau experts are further predicting that in another five years only 50 percent of the American workforce will be employees. We are seeing an explosion of new work models, including consultants, independent contractors, electronic immigrants, teleworkers, and contingency laborers. While in past years entrepreneurs were expected to rent buildings and hire employees, these days they may operate Internet businesses that require neither. Today's temps may work from home and design their own schedules. These are not the characteristics of the workplace we were led to expect by our parents and grandparents. These are not the kinds of workplaces where the loyalty of a company guarantees us a weekly paycheck in exchange for our time.

If terms like *contingency worker* or *temp* sound unappealing, you can create your own. What would you like to be called? How about "creative," "free," "imaginative," "innovative," "original," "ingenious," "inspired," "pioneering," "groundbreaking," or "clever"? Why don't you create your own original word for your ideal work environment?

A few years ago I decided that instead of *entrepreneur*, the term

Eaglepreneur had a nicer ring to it and accentuated the way I differ from a traditional entrepreneur. I liked many aspects of what is implied by the term *entrepreneur*, but I did not envision myself as another Bill Gates or Sam Walton or dream of managing twenty thousand employees. I enjoy working independently and making my own decisions, but I'd rather not be bogged down by the traditional business elements of a bricks-and-mortar establishment with employees, leases, and sign permits. Therefore, I decided I was an Eaglepreneur. Go ahead, check it out—http://www.eaglepreneur.com—I have the domain. I claimed that title, and you can do the same with your own. As a Revolutionary, you too will recognize the new opportunities to custom-build your own fulfilling work.

Yes, the workplace is changing—and yes, the career ladder is broken. Today's career path may look more like a labyrinth, in which every time you thought you were heading straight toward the goal, you reach a turn in the road and need to change direction to continue your progress.

It's initially frightening, of course, but only before you consider the payoff. These days, you can build skills and competence in

> **Revolutionary Insight**
>
> *Chain Saw Consultant*
>
> This is an actual term being used for a consultant hired specifically to reduce employee head count, allowing the company's top executives to remain blameless. (See http://www.wordspy.com/words/chainsaw consultant.asp.)

one job and move along to a new company, confident that you are still on the right path. But forget about moving up one notch each year in your current company—it may not happen. You can also forget about being rewarded just because you've been around one more year. Few people are being rewarded for longevity. The only things that get rewarded in today's workplace are *results*.

Yes, millions of Americans have found this new way of working intimidating and unexpected. This giant tidal wave of change has swept over their lives, frequently not taking them *toward* their dreams but setting them *back,* sometimes tragically. Rather than the pleasant retirement they anticipated, they have been confronted with downsizing, outsourcing, reengineering, mergers, acquisitions, and restructuring. Seniority is no longer valued, and common benefits like health insurance are disappearing, even in the jobs that do remain.

As I wrote about in my previous book, *48 Days to the Work You Love,* many people have felt victimized by these workplace changes. ATMs are doing the work of 179,000 former bank tellers, sight-recognition machines have replaced 47,000 postal workers, and self-scanning systems now help you check out at the grocery store without the need for a friendly cashier. Apparel workers and financial analysts have been coerced into training their foreign counterparts who will work for a fraction of the hourly wage expected in America. Also in this group are the 33,000 General Motors employees who have been told their jobs will be eliminated. Volkswagen is predicting the elimination of 20,000 jobs; at the time of this writing, Ford is threatening to cut 40,000 positions, Chrysler 14,500, and Mercedes 6,000. No one is immune from the changes that face us every day.

There is another important reason that work needs to be redefined: Today we're all looking for more than just a paycheck. We have philosophical and spiritual questions that challenge our workplace contentment. With all the uncertainty in the workplace and the uncertainty in our world in general, I find that more people than ever before are looking for ways to contribute—to make a difference, to make the world a better place, to do something noble, to make sure they are living out the purpose for their lives by doing work that really matters.

Fortunately, the unexpected opportunities for doing just that are astounding. Thanks to the Internet, the ease of communication around the world, and the growth of service and information computer applications, it's never been easier to start a small business and run it from home with virtually no overhead. People are finding a new affirmation of right-brain skills and the profitability of artistic, creative, and compassionate skills.

Here are just a few examples of some Revolutionaries I've met lately who never could have done what they're doing in previous eras but who are thriving today. At a recent corporate party, a gentleman drew a quick caricature of my wife and me, telling us he gets a hundred dollars an hour for doing what he loves to do. Every Friday our masseuse arrives at our house, providing our massages in a manner convenient for us and with no rent or utility costs for her. A recent client decided to forgo traditional publishing and instead write an e-book; he now nets in excess of ten thousand dollars a month, with no printing or shipping charges. A young man just completed a stamped concrete sidewalk at our country house. Although he has only a high school diploma, I paid him as much as I'd have paid a highly trained professional for his unique ability.

And in my own business, I'm constantly on the lookout for new ways to grow and reach more people. I recently experimented with a teleseminar, giving a talk on a niche topic to students from around the world who participated without the obstacles of travel and hotel expenses. I put on my blue jeans, baseball cap, and a headset, and after a mere seventy-minute presentation deposited eighteen thousand dollars in my bank account.

These and other revolutionary work models aren't just providing us with exciting and fulfilling new career paths. As a (perhaps surprising) added benefit, they are raising our standards of living. People often assume that if they follow their dreams or do something more creative and less traditional, they will have to adjust to a meager income. Most of us assume, for instance, that if we were in "full-time ministry" we would have to adjust to living on beans and rice. However, in my observation and personal experience, I have seen the opposite—following one's dreams, calling, or ministry typically releases not only a new sense of peace, meaning, and accomplishment but also a financial windfall.

The Bible gives dignity to any honest work. There are few non-sacred occupations. The idea of being "called to ministry or

Outrageous Outsourcing

We've all heard about the jobs going to India and China. Well, here's an even more imposing proposition. A California company plans to anchor a six-hundred-cabin cruise ship just beyond the three-mile limit off the coast of El Segundo, near Los Angeles, and fill it with foreign software programmers. The company will classify the workers as seamen and thus avoid U.S. payroll taxes and the need for visas. The programmers will work eight- or ten-hour shifts, day or night, and receive about $21,500 a year. I can't decide whether to admire the company's creativity or be outraged by its audacity.

POT-SHOTS
Brilliant Thoughts in 17 Words or Less

© ASHLEIGH BRILLIANT 1931.   POT-SHOTS NO. 5347.

YOU ARE NOW LEAVING THE PAST AND ENTERING THE FUTURE:

BE
PREPARED
FOR
UNEXPECTED
EVENTS.

Ashleigh Brilliant
SANTA BARBARA

full-time service" is simply a cultural misrepresentation of God's view of meaningful work. We need to eliminate the artificial ranking that assigns a higher degree of godliness to certain types of work. There are no second-class citizens in the workplace. I thank God for the talents of our lawn-maintenance man, and I'm touched deeply when I see the beauty he creates in the grass, flowers, and trees surrounding our home. Fulfilling our unique calling will be expressed in a wide variety of applications in the work we do. Don't assume that only church-paid positions provide

Revolutionary Insight

Tabula Rasa—The Power of a Clean Slate

Tabula rasa is a Latin term meaning "clean slate." Now, I know this may sound intimidating when we're talking about a career path. After all, many of us have been trained to think of our careers—and our lives—as linear progressions. We go to school to learn certain skills to benefit us in a particular trade or profession. Who wants to start a new career path from scratch once they've laid the foundation for what they thought was a predictable one? Well, the most successful people usually view change differently.

It was a cold December night in West Orange, New Jersey. Thomas Edison's factory was humming with activity. Work was proceeding on a variety of fronts as the great inventor was trying to turn more of his dreams into practical realities.

Edison's plant, made of concrete and steel, was deemed fireproof. As you may have already guessed, it wasn't! On that frigid night in 1914, the sky was lit up by a sensational blaze that had burst through the plant roof.

Edison's twenty-four-year-old son, Charles, made a frenzied search for his father. When Charles finally found him, the famous inventor was watching the fire. His white hair was blowing in the wind, and his face was illuminated by the leaping flames. "My heart ached for him," said Charles. "Here he was, sixty-seven years old, and everything he had worked for was going up in flames. When he saw me, he shouted, 'Charles! Where's your mother?' When I told him I didn't know, he said, 'Find her! Bring her here! She'll never see anything like this as long as she lives.' "

The next morning, Mr. Edison looked at the ruins of his factory and said this of his loss: "There's value in disaster. All our mistakes are burned up. Thank God, we can start anew."

What a wonderful perspective on an event that at first glance seemed disastrous! A job loss, a business failure, a personal dream gone sour—whether these things destroy an individual depends largely on the attitude he or she takes toward them. When you're faced with your own disaster, sort out why the misfortune happened and learn something from it. Think of different approaches that can be taken the next time. With any failure, there is a lesson to be learned and forgiveness to be found. Wipe the slate clean and look forward. Start over. Be wiser and humbler in view of what has happened, but don't stop living because of it.

Don't ignore the value of your tabula rasa.

opportunities to do godly work. Humanitarian, non-profit, and ministry work opportunities are exploding—and they don't require a poverty-level income.

Telecommuting allows today's workers to make big-city money while living high in the hills of Colorado. Virtual businesses allow shoestring operations to compete with traditional bricks-and-mortar businesses, without the hassle of overhead expenses.

And the opportunities aren't limited to those of us who want to strike out on our own. In the past ten years, there has been a 96 percent increase in the number of American workers who have negotiated flexible work schedules. John Challenger, of the outplacement consulting firm Challenger, Gray & Christmas, recently reported that 29 percent of the workforce has a lot of say in where and when they work. JetBlue Airways may be the ultimate example. All of the airline's one thousand reservations agents work from computers in their homes.

With advances in technology and a shrinking skilled labor pool, companies can look anywhere in the world for workers. You can complain about "all the jobs going to India" or be thrilled that now you can live on top of a mountain in Woodland Park, Colorado, and still be integrally involved in the day-to-day operations of a great company (as my son Kevin is). Thanks to satellite Internet reception, he can run with the elk in the morning, teach his kids to fly-fish at midday, and be on a national conference call that afternoon—all with no commute to the office or compromise in compensation.

Make no mistake about it, change of all kinds—economic, social, cultural, technological, and political—is not merely accelerating but exploding. And the rate of change shows no sign of slowing in our lifetime. *Capitalism and free enterprise have fueled the new opportunities—and also widened the chasm between those who cling to the past and those who welcome the inevitable changes.*

No More Dreaded Mondays will put you in the driver's seat to understand, embrace, and profit from these inevitable changes.

> Failure is the opportunity to begin again more intelligently.
>
> —Henry Ford

Don't Be "Stupid"!

As the United States has become more industrially and technologically advanced, we have confused bigger with better, more work with more success, and in the process lost many simple pleasures. Too often we see our work as little more than the means to a paycheck—a boring, repetitive process devoid of any real challenge and appealing engagement.

As far back as 1776, Adam Smith saw the dangers of moving in this direction. In his highly influential *Wealth of Nations,* he wrote that a person who spends his life performing the same repetitive tasks "generally becomes as stupid and ignorant as it is possible for a human creature to become." Wow! Now, that's not a pretty picture. Unfortunately, much of our work today consists of those boring, repetitive tasks. But those of us doing these tasks are not only in danger of extreme boredom; we are also highly at risk for being replaced by computers, by new technologies, or by people somewhere in the world willing to work for lower wages. And we are at risk of losing touch with our sense of God's calling.

Let me assure you, this is not a time to move backward or to discard the many advances in work models and options. I am writing to assure you that *business is not declining and opportunities are not diminishing. However, they most surely are changing.*

We have seen similar changes and transformations as we moved from the Agricultural Age to the Industrial Age to the Technological Age to the Information Age and now to the Idea Age. Just as we have seen transitions from production work to knowledge work, we are now moving into an era that embraces "high concept" and "high touch" models of work. In place of the left-brain skills that were so crucial in the dawn of the Information Age, we are seeing empathy, joyfulness, storytelling, and caring as the defining characteristics of those who are flourishing and prospering today. If you have a heart of compassion and a desire to bring healing to the world, today may be the most opportune time in history for you to fulfill that passion.

In today's work arena, creativity may be more of an asset than competence.

Competence may imply arriving on time, doing what's expected, and being a loyal employee. It may mean having an appropriate degree and being certified to complete a series of tasks. Yet thousands of workers with all of those characteristics have found that they have been summarily replaced or simply eliminated, often with little compensation or advance notice. Creativity does not come from special intelligence or training—rather, it comes from listening to what you already know, looking at yourself, and recognizing common solutions to new challenges. Most

---

Honey, I Got Fired

Nathaniel Hawthorne went home to tell his wife that he had just been fired from his job. "Good," she said. "Now you can write your book." "What do we live on meanwhile?" Hawthorne asked. His wife opened a drawer filled with money. "I have always known that you are a man of genius," she said. "So I saved a little each week, and now I have enough to last for a year." Hawthorne used the time to write *The Scarlet Letter*, one of the great masterpieces of American literature.

of us have creative ideas every day, in the shower, on a walk with our kids, or during a boring meeting. Now is the time to embrace those ideas and act on them.

I have a friend whose husband came home with a red computer button and casually asked her, "What can we do with this?" Together, they turned it into a gag gift item (PANIC button) and have sold over 130,000 without any paid advertising. Soon thereafter, they developed "the lowest cost PC (Pencil Computer) on the Planet." They state that you can brag that this PC is "crash proof, never gets viruses, never needs to reboot, and is wireless." And, yes, they've sold over 100,000 ordinary pencils in little plastic bags that announce their wonderful features. (See http://www.panicbuttons.com.)

I urge you to stop looking at today's changes as threats and start seeing them rather as opportunities. As Napoleon Hill wrote in 1937 in his classic book, *Think and Grow Rich*, "With every change, there are the equal seeds of opportunity."

Throughout history, society's problem solvers have been generously rewarded for their efforts. Eli Whitney invented the cotton gin. But the Eli Whitneys of the world didn't add to unemployment; they stimulated the development of new and fulfilling opportunities as people were absorbed into the next equally fulfilling and prosperous chapter in American history. Repeatedly I hear from people eighteen months after they were fired that losing their jobs was "the best thing that ever happened" to them.

Ready for a Change? This Book Is for You!

Today's best opportunities may not include punching a clock, having a company car, or being provided health insurance and a retirement plan. They may not involve an eight-to-five schedule or even the need to go to an office. While this may be frightening to you if you have never experienced anything else, recognize that these opportunities are more exciting, personally fulfilling, and financially rewarding than any of the predictable jobs of the last hundred years.

> *Oh, you hate your job? Why didn't you say so?*
> *There's a support group for that. It's called everybody,*
> *and they meet at the bar.*
>
> —Drew Carey

If you are a baby boomer (born between 1946 and 1964), you may never have experienced anything other than the "go to work—get paid" model. Fortunately, it's never too late to stretch your thinking. You are about to see a variety of examples of the coming models of work. While retirement may be expected at age sixty-two, you may be one of the many who want or need to continue in fulfilling and profitable work. No problem—you will see the variety of ways you can do exactly that. And you don't have to beg for a paycheck for that to happen.

If you're a member of Generation X (born between 1965 and 1981), you may already have seen parents lose their jobs after twenty-five years of faithful service and through no fault of their

Revolutionary Insight

Reframing—A New Way of Thinking

No, I'm not going to offer instruction on how to build your house again. *Reframing* is a term used in Neuro-Linguistic Programming that refers to the process of seeing things, problems, situations, or people in new ways. Psychologists frequently help their patients reframe negative thoughts or beliefs by connecting them with positive experiences. But there are many ways to use this technique in every area of our lives. For example, if you imagine a computer keyboard with a new layout, then you've just reframed the idea that the current model is the best there is. Travel in England and drive on the "wrong" side of the road and you've reframed your normal experience of highway travel. Dream up a life in which you never want to retire and you've reframed your normal way of thinking. There is a story of the Peruvian Indians who, upon seeing the sails of their Spanish invaders coming in from the sea, attributed the sight to a mirage or freakish weather and went about their business. They had never seen a sailing vessel before, so they screened out what did not fit their previous experience. Rather than reframing their limited experience to include scenarios they'd never imagined possible, they allowed their conquerors to approach unhindered.

To think of your job as two thousand hours of work in a year rather than fifty weeks of forty hours a week opens up the opportunity of reframing. Another way of reframing your notion of work is to recognize that you may be able to do some of your work at home, in a lake cabin, or while writing a book or spending time with your family.

I worked with Jane to help her reframe her concerns about a teaching position in interior design she'd been offered. Yes, they still want a minimum of forty hours a week, but she will be going to campus only three days a week for two semesters and only two days during the summer. She can devote a great deal of her time to her own practice and the professional organizations of her choosing. Meanwhile, the university will be funding the industry-related research she'd wanted to do for a long time and has offered her a generous allowance to decorate her office. All this in addition to a "full-time" salary package. This is just one example of reframing a "normal" opportunity and recognizing its potential to allow you to do extraordinary things.

How can you reframe your ideas about work and life? Rather than feeling you have a diminishing ability to contribute, perhaps you could take a cue from the movement from production work to knowledge work and think of yourself as moving from "energy" to "wisdom," thereby increasing your value.

own. Your generation is more receptive to building a career path around your areas of competence, but keep in mind that the application of those skills may change as you move from one company to another or even branch out on your own. You are likely looking for a new kind of work—a work model that allows flexibility, embraces family and other personal values, yet connects with a larger sense of purpose. *No More Dreaded Mondays* is your window into the Ideas Age and the resulting "green" businesses, humanitarianism, social entrepreneurship, and ministry opportunities.

> *You can't sail to new lands unless you're willing to lose sight of the shore.*

If you are a Millennial (born since 1981), you are a member of an incredibly sociable, talented, open-minded, influential, and achievement-oriented generation. But you probably have little interest in being tied down by an eight-to-five schedule. Companies are scrambling to design work environments for recruiting, managing, motivating, and retaining you and your peers. But this book will also confirm the many choices you have for *creating* your own version of meaningful work.

If you are an executive or small business owner looking to streamline your business, this book will show you new options for compensating for results, rather than guarantees for time alone. Perhaps you would like the services of a brilliant graphic designer, accountant, salesperson, or web team without the obligation of salaries and benefit packages. Yes, you can reduce your exposure and fixed expenses while still rewarding those who bring value to your company's goals.

If you are a manager hoping to inspire your employees, *No More Dreaded Mondays* will help you match those individuals with positions that release their strongest areas of competence—and thus equip them for peak performance and yourself for managerial excellence.

If you are a university career center director or high school guidance counselor, this book will provide a road map for helping your students recognize what work skills the world really needs. We already know that, ten years after graduation, 80 percent of college graduates are doing something totally unconnected to their degrees. And that's okay. We have to understand that a college degree is part of the maturation process. It helps broaden horizons, but it may do little to prepare for the actual work required for success ten or twenty years later.

Whether you love your current job or loathe it, are hoping to start a new business or better manage your current one, *No More Dreaded Mondays* can help you find, or create, more meaningful, fulfilling, and profitable work.

> The real act of discovery is not in finding new lands,
> but in seeing with new eyes.
>
> —Marcel Proust

Get ready to open your eyes!

If You're a Revolutionary, You Will

- Approach the inevitable changes with excited anticipation rather than intimidating, crippling fear.
- Understand how to create continuity in your life while navigating work-life changes.
- Learn that the goal is not to maintain predictable levels of accomplishment but to open the door to higher levels of success than you ever thought possible.
- Leave mediocrity behind and rise above the day-to-day existence of the average person.
- Move forward expecting to more completely fulfill your calling and to *increase* your time freedom, sense of purpose, and income!

2

LET YOUR LIFE SPEAK

Are you making the most of the life you have? Does your daily work shout out to the world the very purpose for your being? If people watched you on Monday morning, would they see evidence of your true *genius*? Would they see you carrying out your *mission* and fulfilling your *destiny*? Are your moment-by-moment activities accurate expressions of your *calling*?

I believe every one of us has a unique *calling*. It's certainly not something reserved for a chosen few who end up as pastors, priests, or monks. We all fulfill that calling by being excellent as we express our talents and abilities, and our dreams and passions. Anyone can do a job, but a calling is lived out by a person who has tapped into wisdom that goes beyond education and intelligence.

Work that's connected to your calling is never done only as an exchange for a paycheck. Living out your mission on earth by answering your calling should also provide a sense of being connected to a higher purpose. If your work is boring, exhausting, and monotonous, you are clearly unconnected to your calling. And if that's true for you, it's my belief that this book will help you connect with your calling. If you've already found the work that you believe you are here on earth to do, then *No More Dreaded Mondays* will explain how to better integrate your work with the other aspects of your life, so that you have more time to spend with the people you love or on the hobbies that bring you peace and fulfillment.

Every day, millions of people rush to get to jobs they don't love and then go home to lives that are equally empty and boring. And yet those people defend their choices as responsible, practical, and realistic. How can it be responsible to live lives devoid of meaning, joy, and purpose?

Pray devoutly and hammer stoutly.

—English proverb

Carol is a Los Angeles media executive. At forty-six years old, she has reached the pinnacle of her career, with a world-class apartment and a beach house for fun and relaxation. However, although her income puts her in the top 1 percent of the nation, she feels no sense of fulfillment from her work. Thanks to her busy schedule, she hasn't been to her beach house in over a year or had the time to develop any close relationships. Moreover, she's feeling the pressure at work to make way for younger and more attractive personalities. She dreads Monday mornings because they have come to mean tackling a frantic surge of tasks that are heavy on short-term urgency but light on long-term significance. In taking a long overdue look at where she is and where she is going, Carol identified one of her goals as being "to smile more on my way to happiness."

A story is told of a South American tribe that went on a long journey; they'd walk for days without stopping, then all of a sudden stop, sit down to rest, and make camp for a couple of days before going any farther. They explained to Westerners that they needed the time of rest so that their souls could catch up with them.

What about you? Are you working so hard you've forgotten to let your soul catch up now and then? Are you feeling like your work is soul-less and little more than a method of producing a paycheck?

POT-SHOTS
Brilliant Thoughts in 17 Words or Less

POT-SHOTS NO. 2592.

I WOULD
LIKE TO SPEAK
TO WHOEVER
IS IN CONTROL
OF MY LIFE,

AND SUGGEST
SOME
IMPROVEMENTS.

Ashleigh
Brilliant

©ASHLEIGH BRILLIANT 1983.

In the busyness of modern life, I fear many of us have lost the rhythm between activity and rest. Just as exhaling without occasionally inhaling will cause a person to turn blue and pass out, busyness without rest will cause you to pass out on the things that matter. "I am so busy." We say this as a badge of honor, as if our exhaustion were a trophy and our ability to withstand seventy- to eighty-hour workweeks a mark of real character. We convince ourselves that the busier we are, the more we are accomplishing and the more important we must be. But is this really so? Does more activity really mean more accomplishment? To be unavailable to friends and family, to miss the sunsets and the full moons, to blast through all our obligations without time for taking a deep breath—are these really the marks of a successful life?

In a recent issue of Rick Warren's ministry newsletter, the author of *The Purpose Driven Life* was talking about our need to maintain a necessary buffer time in our life. Warren used as his basis the following verse from Ecclesiastes: "Only someone too stupid to find his way home would wear himself out with work" (10:15, TEV). How do you like that? Have you been worn out at work lately? If you have, did you know that you've been put in the category of being "too stupid to find his way home"? Maybe that wording is a little harsher than it was intended to be, and perhaps you can find softer language in another Bible translation. But I like the message of this verse. Don't wear yourself out so much with working that you're no good for anything else.

If you are losing your leisure, look out. You may be losing your soul.

—Logan Pearsall Smith (1865–1946)

Make it a habit to embrace Sabbath days and times in your life. Wisdom, peace, contentment, and insight about investing your life in fulfilling work will grow in those times. Take a walk; give thanks for simple things; take a bath with music playing and candles burning; turn off the telephone, pager, television, and computer. Carve out those times for restoration and spiritual breathing. Even Jesus got away from the crowds periodically.

Let me ask you this: What is your life saying to the world? Are you living your life too small? Is it so full of meaningless tasks that there's no room left for the things that make your heart sing? Are you pushing so hard in *doing* more that you have lost the sense of *being* more? Does more activity really equal greater accomplishment, or does it at some point tip the scale and begin to diminish the meaning of your life? Are you creating the legacy you want to leave for your loved ones?

Do You Have a Calling—Or Just a Job?

We all have unique *abilities* and *skills*. You may be a gifted communicator or a caring coworker and friend, a good decision maker or a talented salesperson. So why are many of us frustrated in applying those abilities? Isn't that enough, to have the *ability* to do something well? The answer to that question is a resounding *no!* If you are operating on your abilities alone, you will likely never feel that sense of fulfillment, meaning, and accomplishment that all people want.

Think of your *calling* as the big picture that many people forget to keep in mind when mapping out their careers and their lives. It's your calling that makes a difference in your life, that builds meaning for you. Those of us who follow our callings can look back at our lives in later years to see the impact we've made on the world.

The author Stephen Covey says that we all want "to live, to love, to learn and to leave a legacy."[1] There's no better way to leave a legacy than by following our calling. A legacy connects with our spiritual need to have a sense of meaning, purpose, and contribution. Our work is not just something we have to do. Rather, it is our best opportunity to answer our calling each day, and ultimately to leave a legacy. People won't remember your financial worth for long, but they'll remember what you did that had lasting value.

The word *vocation* comes from the Latin *vocare,* which means "to call." It suggests that you are listening for something that is calling out to you, listening for God's voice—something that is particular to you. A calling is something you have to listen for— a connection to something larger than yourself.

In a world shaken by terrorism, natural disasters, and the uncertainty of everyday existence, it is hardly surprising that so many of us are searching for some sense of mission or calling in our work today. We've realized that there is more to life than mortgages and car payments. We're searching for a connection to something that "makes a difference," that somehow improves the world or has a noble cause. If our celebrities and business leaders can give back to society, there has to be more that each of us can do.

But what? Where do we begin? I would suggest that you look at what you most enjoy—what do you do with *enthusiasm*? Keep in mind that the word *enthusiasm* comes from the Greek *en theos* and literally means "God in us." You don't have to be religious to realize that true enthusiasm is about more than fun and games. It comes from deep within and connects us to what is meaningful, purposeful, and eternal.

As Frederick Buechner said, "The place God calls you to is the place where your deep gladness and the world's deep hunger meet." Ask yourself: What is the world hungering for right now? How can I use my unique skills and talents to satisfy that hunger? Don't rest until you find your own answer.

As I first wrote in my previous book, *48 Days to the Work You Love,* jobs will come and go, but that should never deter you from your *calling*. Any work you commit yourself to must blend the following three areas:

1. SKILLS AND ABILITIES. Yes, you must have the ability to do your job, but keep in mind that skill or ability alone will not necessarily lead to a sense of purpose and fulfillment.

2. PERSONALITY TENDENCIES. How do you relate to other people? In what kinds of environments are you most comfortable? Are you expressive and visionary, or are you analytical, logical, and detailed? Knowing your strongest personality traits is the first step toward finding authentic, meaningful, and enjoyable work.

3. VALUES, DREAMS, AND PASSIONS. What do you most enjoy doing? If money were not a concern, how would you spend your time? What themes do you keep coming back to? What activities did you enjoy as a child but perhaps were told were unrealistic or impractical to focus on as a career?[2]

Where the spirit does not work with the hand there is no art.

—Leonardo da Vinci

Finding work that's in line with our skills, our personality, and our interests seems logical enough and yet is a tough concept for many of us to grasp. There is a subtle cultural and spiritual misperception that makes us believe that following our natural inclinations and pursuing our dreams is somehow selfish, egotistical, and financially impractical. However, my experience shows that the reverse is true. Those whose work is not an authentic fit frequently struggle to maintain financial solvency and are plagued with unhappiness. One of my clients, a doctor, desperately wants to be involved in humanitarian educational projects, yet he feels forced to continue practicing medicine to provide for his family. But rather than making the comfortable $250,000 income his specialty should generate, he struggles to keep up a low six-figure income and hates the demands of being expected to continue in the field of his academic training. Another client of mine had been told for years to be realistic about the fact that his artwork would never pay the bills. As a result, he traded in his brush and easel for a job in hotel management. Yet, with my encouragement, he transitioned into working on his art full-time. He now not only enjoys his own authentic work but has increased his income tenfold.

If we are unfaithful to ourselves, we are detracting not only from our own peace and accomplishment but from those around us as well. As the thirteenth-century Sufi poet Rumi said, "If you are here unfaithfully with us, you're causing terrible damage."[3] An integral part of the process is to recognize where you are naturally *en theos* (in God)—*enthusiastic.*

For the person seeking to walk in God's will, work should be meaningful and an expression of who you are. "Calling" is not an external voice forcing you to be something you are not. Rather, it is an authentic alignment of how God has gifted you in (1) skills and abilities; (2) personality traits; and (3) values, dreams, and passions. The apostle Peter wrote: "God has given each of you some special abilities; be sure to use them to help each other, passing on to others God's many kinds of blessings" (1 Peter 4:10, TLB).

Life is much too short for shallow interests and shallow passions. Only by staying true to your unique dreams and calling will you ultimately believe that yours was a life well lived.

The mass of men lead lives of quiet desperation. What is called resignation is confirmed desperation.

—Henry David Thoreau

When we spend forty to fifty hours a week doing something that is unconnected to our calling, we're miserable not just at work but at home as well. Our remaining discretionary hours are often filled with futile attempts to reclaim our spiritual wholeness and may simply frustrate us and drive us further from our true mission. When you add up the time we spend with our families and friends, exercising and doing household chores, cooking and eating—not to mention sleeping—it's easy to see how weeks, even months can pass without devoting any time to ourselves and our purpose in life. No wonder so many of us hate Mondays—just when we've shaken the previous workweek and started to think about ourselves and our goals, another workweek begins! But be confident there is more to your life than beating the competition, meeting deadlines, increasing shareholder wealth, and grabbing your paycheck at the end of one more hectic week; it's just a matter of figuring out what you really want to do and pursuing it with focus and determination.

There is an old story about Quaker relief workers in Europe after World War II. After receiving help from the workers, a refugee asked what Quakers believe. When a few of the Quakers explained that they believed helping people with their physical needs was the most spiritual thing they could do, the woman broke out in a smile and said, "You Quakers ought to preach what you practice." Of course, in keeping with their simple way of life, the Quakers felt it was more important to live one's faith than to preach it, which is why one of their most profound and well-known statements is "Let your life speak." This command urges us to live life authentically, to make sure our daily actions display our values and deepest beliefs. What does your current work say about your life? If you don't like what it's saying, why not give some thought to what you'd rather be doing instead?

Francis of Assisi counseled his brothers: "Preach the gospel at all times. If necessary, use words."

What do your daily actions say about your beliefs? Are your highest values and ideals guiding everything you do? Or do you save your best self for the activities away from work? There's a strong tendency among Americans to separate our work life from our "real" life. We work because we have to, so then we can spend the weekend doing what we *really* want to do. Or we strive—in an attempt to please God—to do what we consider *really* important (separate from the realm of work). We divide work and play as opposites—and long for playtime to arrive in the hope that it will erase the memory of work. We create an artificial dichotomy: we feel we are pleasing God on the weekend, but the rest of the week—well, that's "just" our work. Even all our fantasies about retirement make it clear that many of us seek to eliminate work as quickly as possible so that we can experience what we anticipate will be day upon day of uninterrupted play. But is the only goal of our working life to get to the point when we can finally stop working? If so, then it confirms the picture that work is just a bitter pill to be endured until the moment we can escape it. Those conflicting opposites compete for our time and energy.

But this attitude will make it impossible for you to enjoy an integrated, wholesome life. What so many of us see as opposites are really parts of the same healthy unity. All around us in nature we see the paradox of opposites that do not negate each other but rather work together to create a mysterious wholeness that makes each part better and more appreciated. The darkness of winter and the new birth of spring, the feelings of happiness and despair, the states of waking and sleep all complement each other, resulting in a richness that gives life its true depth. In the words of Thomas Merton: "There is in all visible things . . . a hidden wholeness."[4] Merton explains that these apparent opposites actually *need* each other in order to exist, and were it not for each opposing force, we could never truly appreciate the balance and complexity of our world. But in a culture that prefers either-or solutions, we look for ways to eliminate work in favor of play, without realizing the two can—and should—coexist.

We want light without darkness, spring growth without the harshness of winter's death, joy with no sadness, money with no effort, and play without work. But as long as we see work as a necessary evil to be escaped as quickly as possible, as long as we believe the work experience cannot be fulfilling, rewarding, and purposeful, we view it with jaundiced eyes and lose the potential to spend the majority of our time accomplishing the mission of our lives.

> If we had no winter, the spring would not be so pleasant:
> if we did not sometimes taste adversity,
> prosperity would not be so welcome.
>
> —Anne Bradstreet

Just Doing My Job!

Too often I hear people tell me they work for companies they really don't believe in or make products they would not recommend to their friends. Just doing a job cannot justify doing something unethical, immoral, dishonest, or in conflict with your values. Guards in the German concentration camps, even after forming friendships with the Jewish prisoners, would often justify walking them to the gas chambers with the statement "I'm just doing my job." This is an extreme example, but it shows how dangerous it can be to justify unethical, immoral, and even evil behavior with the statement "I'm just doing my job." Unfortunately, I still see people who are selling cars they know are defective, products that don't deliver, food they know is unhealthy, "resort" land that is nothing but swamps, dental work that isn't necessary, financial figures that are not quite accurate, and "business opportunities" that don't really work. A manager from a financial services company wrote me that he had just taken the wedding rings off a young couple's hands when they were late with a payment and that he had started repossession proceedings for a gentleman's prosthetic leg. When describing his work, he said, "My soul is being stripped from me."

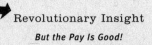

Revolutionary Insight

But the Pay Is Good!

When I take on new clients, I ask them to describe briefly their current work situations. Here's the written response from a female executive who had been employed by a government agency for nine years: "Intolerable, evil, degrading, dirty, backbreaking, dehumanizing, demoralizing, but the pay is good." She, like many of us, came to the realization that money is ultimately never enough compensation for an investment of our time and energy. We also need a sense of meaning, accomplishment, and purpose.

Carl Jung, the psychoanalyst, said we go through seasons in our lives. In the first seasons, we are more concerned with physical, material needs—food on the table, roof over our heads, et cetera. In the later seasons, we traditionally start asking questions like: Is there really a purpose for my life? Am I making a difference? How will I be remembered? But in today's volatile environment, many of us, even those in the early seasons of life, are asking the big philosophical and spiritual questions. These questions require different kinds of answers. Fortunately, there does not have to be a trade-off. Doing something that is "noble" or something that makes a difference does not necessarily mean that you will lower your income. In fact, I usually see that when there is an authentic alignment of our natural talents, more money comes our way. My good friend Dave Ramsey suffered a crushing financial disaster at age twenty-six, when he thought he was at the top of his real estate game. But he took that experience, combined with some good old-fashioned soul-searching, and redirected it into helping others avoid financial disasters. As a result, he has become a millionaire many times over.

As I have discovered from my years of coaching experience, the best way to make money is to do something you love and do it with excellence. And it should come as no surprise that it's harder to make money doing something you don't enjoy. Finding your purpose or mission in life not only brings a sense of fulfillment and accomplishment but releases self-confidence, boldness, and enthusiasm—three key ingredients for any moneymaking endeavor.

If the pay is the only thing keeping you in your job, you are likely sacrificing your health, your confidence, your enthusiasm—and a higher level of income.

What is it that you've been justifying doing just because it's "part of your job"? Having the ability to do something well is not enough reason to continue doing it—especially if it violates your values and common sense. If your work doesn't express your values, you're setting up the possibility for unethical behavior to creep into other areas of your life. And ulcers, migraines, and other stress-related illnesses are frequent side effects of living a less than authentic life. Scientists like Dr. Esther Sternberg, director of the Integrative Neuroimmune Program at the National Institute of Mental Health (NIMH), have identified the effects of stress at work caused by lack of fit or mismatched passions. She states that such stress can "result in autoimmune diseases like rheumatoid arthritis, lupus, or other autoimmune diseases." Other indicators of a stress-filled life listed by the NIMH are difficulty sleeping, changes in appetite, panic attacks, gastrointestinal problems, and prolonged feelings of sadness or worthlessness.[5]

In the movie *Cool Hand Luke*, as a guard beats a prisoner only to create fear in the other inmates, he says, "I'm just doing my job. You gotta appreciate that." And Paul Newman's character responds: "Nah. Calling it your job don't make it right, boss." I agree.

A man had better starve at once than lose his innocence in the process of getting his bread.

—Henry David Thoreau

Now, what about those of you working for "good" companies doing important, "meaningful" work who still feel something's missing? Or you may be in a "ministry" position but still feel frustrated due to draining, unfulfilling work. Well, guess what? Doing work that is seen as noble, humanitarian, or altruistic can be just as damaging if it is not an authentic fit for you. I have seen countless people over the years attempt to do work that seemed meaningful but was not an authentic fit for them. I've seen missionaries come home in defeat, pastors battling with ulcers and migraines, and community volunteers who ended up jaded and bitter because of their recipients' lack of gratitude. If you try to do something noble that has no connection to who you are, you may impress others for a time. But if you are not embracing your unique abilities, you soon find yourself drained both emotionally and physically. You may do more damage than good. When you attempt to do something that is unconnected to your talents, your interests, and your values, you can expend all the energy in the world and still feel unsatisfied.

As I grow older I pay less attention to what men say. I just watch what they do.

—Andrew Carnegie

In a Dark Wood?

"Midway on our life's journey, I found myself in dark woods, the right road lost. To tell about those woods is hard—so tangled and rough and savage that thinking of it now, I feel the old fear stirring . . . Death is hardly more bitter."[6] Thus begins the *Inferno*, the first part of Dante's famous epic poem, *The Divine Comedy*. Literature, art, and Hollywood movies are full of the theme that life is a journey, a personal pilgrimage, and we're all at some unknown point between the beginning and the end of it. Today's downsizings, layoffs, loss of pension plans, outsourcing of jobs, or even the general sense of being off track are forcing many to make sudden changes in their career paths. I am seeing increased numbers of physicians, dentists, attorneys, pastors, marketing professionals, salespeople, teachers, IT professionals, and others who are looking at options for career realignment. The angst-filled search for a proper direction is no longer only a strictly midlife endeavor but is common among twenty- and thirty-somethings as well.

Recently a twenty-seven-year-old physician contacted me with a desperate plea for life coaching. His dad had been a physician, and he wanted to prove that he could do the same thing and do it better. At twenty-seven, when he fully realized this was his only motivation for a medical career, he became deeply depressed

POT-SHOTS
Brilliant Thoughts in 17 Words or Less

and attempted suicide. A dramatic redirection was required to embrace his true calling.

Where are you on your life's journey? Dante was thirty-five, the age that turned out to be the exact halfway point of his seventy-year life, when he wrote *The Divine Comedy*. He wasn't exactly optimistic about the options for midlife as he wrote, "Abandon all hope, you who enter."

Wherever you are on your life's journey, I would advise you not to abandon hope. It's a healthy process at any point in life to ask, "Who am I and where am I going?" This question can prompt an exciting process of redirection and lead to new clarity and a new sense of meaning and accomplishment. Companies are always looking for people with great work habits, a clear sense of their abilities, and a desire to learn. And as you will discover throughout these pages, there are a wealth of new opportunities that allow you to do work you love, either on a project basis or by contract—and plenty that allow you to create your own work, perhaps unlike anyone has done before.

"Divine Discontent"

> *Don't ignore a subtle sense of unrest. It may be the key to finding the work and life you love.*

Ralph Waldo Emerson talked about the concept of "divine discontent." Have you ever experienced that subtle sense of being off track? That your life is not following a clear path but is constantly being derailed by circumstances that seem to be beyond your control? I see more and more people who are feeling misplaced, off track, or just like they are not making a difference. Driven by the desire to do something "noble" or "significant," they are leaving behind lucrative positions and successful careers in search of more meaning and fulfillment. How do people leave behind positions or professions that others would view as highly desirable? They discover that something more fulfilling is possible.

> *Restlessness is discontent and discontent is the first necessity of progress. Show me a thoroughly satisfied man and I will show you a failure.*
>
> —Thomas A. Edison

The path toward personal authenticity can lead in many surprising directions. Yes, we do see physicians who left their practices to drive trucks, former pastors who became artists, and accountants who now have landscape businesses. But rest assured the application of authenticity does not always require a downward financial shift. In fact, quite often the opposite is true.

> *Discontent is the first step in the progress*
> *of a man or a nation.*
>
> —Oscar Wilde

Some people struggle, whether they are doing something practical and realistic or humanitarian and godly, because it's not in line with their natural abilities. The income may be significant, but it will come at great cost physically, emotionally, and spiritually. Often when a person moves toward authenticity—a true blend of talents and passions—the result is not only a release in the sense of fulfillment and peace, but also unexpected financial abundance.

A true vocation helps us meet not only our own needs but also the needs of those around us. Have you ever heard friends or acquaintances wishing that someone would just give them a job? Waiting for someone to "give" you a job as a supposed favor is likely to sabotage your search for your calling. You *can* structure your work around your goals, meaningful relationships, and your dreams and passions. Look inward to discover the shape of the work that is fitting for you and then ask yourself how to find a fitting application.

Expect change and workplace volatility to enhance, not diminish, your chances of creating meaningful work. It is typically in the midst of change, even if unwelcomed, that we find our true direction. As Emerson said: "A foolish consistency is the hobgoblin of little minds, adored by little statesmen and philosophers and divines. With consistency a great soul has simply nothing to do."

Boy, Do I Feel Crabby!

I frequently draw from the wisdom of the *Peanuts* comic strip. In one episode, Lucy announces, "Boy, do I feel crabby!"

Her little brother, Linus, is quick to try to rescue his sister. "Maybe I can be of help. Why don't you just take my place here in front of the TV while I go and fix you a nice snack? Sometimes we all need a little pampering to help us feel better." Then Linus brings her a sandwich, a few chocolate chip cookies, and some milk.

"Now is there anything else I can get you?" he asks. "Is there anything I haven't thought of?"

"Yes there's one thing you haven't thought of," Lucy responds. And then she screams in his direction, "I don't want to feel better!"

Lucy exemplifies a characteristic I see in a lot of people. They don't really want to change. Even the most miserable work seems to offer a sense of comfort that makes them reluctant to risk substantial change. We all have things in our histories that we cannot change. We can't change our nationality, our parents, or our previous health problems. But we all have the ability to change our thinking and our attitudes today in order to create a more satisfying tomorrow.

> Take the first step in faith. You don't have to see the whole staircase, just take the first step.
> —Dr. Martin Luther King, Jr.

No one needs to feel trapped in a dead-end job—there are too many choices available. It doesn't matter if you trained to be a plumber, an assembly-line worker, a physician, a dentist, or a schoolteacher. It's never too late to change careers or change things about your current career to make it a better fit. There are enough opportunities to personalize your work and make it the most visible expression of your purpose on earth. Look at the examples in Scripture of people who fulfilled their purpose. Moses had to wait many years before walking into his primary role of leading the children of Israel toward the Promised Land. Joseph went through years of unexplainable "misfortunes" as he prepared to become a world leader. Even Jesus spent the majority of his life on earth behind the scenes as the stage was set for the significant last three years of his life.

If we did all the things we are capable of doing, we would literally astound ourselves.

—Thomas A. Edison

Most of us attach an unrealistic amount of meaning to our jobs. Ironically, although we may see our jobs as merely the means to a paycheck, we are also likely to see them as defining features of who we are. That's why when a job disappears, our immediate response often involves a diminished sense of self-worth and clouded identity. A person without a job is often viewed as someone whose life is on hold. I have seen thousands of clients struggle with these inevitable transitions—often hiding out to keep neighbors or friends from knowing the truth. If we have no identity apart from our jobs, we are truly vulnerable. Recognize that your calling involves more than your job or your work. It is part of your life and as such continues even if your job does not. If you had a fitting occupation as a teacher and then lost your job, your calling would not change. You may begin to look for new ways to be nurturing, encouraging, and empathetic, and in the process find an opportunity as executive director of a new day-care center. But remember, your relationships, health, and personal development are all essential components of a life well lived, so don't lose sight of them in your search for meaningful work.

A gem cannot be polished without friction, nor people perfected without trials.

—Chinese proverb

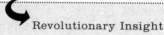

Revolutionary Insight

You Can't Do This

We've all heard about the mom in Florida who lifted a refrigerator off her child and the two neighbors in Canada who lifted a Pontiac Grand Prix off a twenty-seven-year-old mechanic. Stories of extraordinary strength or supernatural ability are common. But here's an interesting twist. In 1977, in Tallahassee, Florida, Laura Shultz picked up the back end of a Buick to get it off her grandson's arm. She was sixty-three at the time and could not recall ever lifting anything heavier than a fifty-pound bag of dog food. Initially, she resisted talking about "the event." Why do you suppose she didn't want to talk about it?

Here's her response in an interview with Dr. Charles Garfield, author of *Peak Performance:* "If I was able to do this when I didn't think I could, what does that say about the rest of my life? Have I wasted it?"

What big goal could you set for yourself, one that would dramatically change your life? Don't put any limitations on your answer. Once you've got it, ask yourself why you picked that goal. Does it go beyond your own needs and desires? *When you have a clear enough "why," you will figure out the "how."* You don't need degrees, training, and a seminar on how to lift a car if your grandchild is trapped underneath one.

Of course, some jobs do require training. And if you weigh 110 pounds and want to play in the NFL, you may need to adjust your goal slightly. You might consider a career as a sports therapist or trainer. The point is, you're never too old to learn something new. After that life-altering event, Laura Shultz decided to go back to school to study geology. She eventually got her degree and went on to teach at a local community college.

What is a goal you would like to accomplish in the next three years? Why do you want that to happen? What are you doing now to make it happen? Don't wait until you're sixty-three to discover your true abilities. And if you are sixty-three, don't be afraid to start now. As the author Barbara Sher says, "It's only too late if you don't start now."

I have always encouraged people to embrace the times "between opportunities." Rather than thinking of themselves as being "off track," "on hold," or "unemployed," I ask people to welcome these interludes as times for restoration, rejuvenation, and clarification.

> *You have a calling which exists only for you*
> *and which only you can fulfill.*
>
> —Dr. Naomi Stephan

If You're a Revolutionary, You Will

- Recognize your life is speaking for you.
- Look for consistency between your "values" and your "actions."
- See that your job is an important subset of your "calling."
- Welcome moments of "divine discontent."
- Expect insights of *en theos* ("enthusiasm").
- Realize that your life up until now may have provided essential preparation for the fulfillment of your calling. It's not too late!

3

WHO'S MAKING YOUR LUNCH TODAY?

In one of my all-time favorite *Peanuts* cartoons, Charlie Brown complains to Linus that every day his lunch is the same. When Linus asks Charlie Brown who makes his lunch, Charlie Brown says, "I do."

When it comes to the activities of our lives, most of us make our own lunches. So while there may be some comfort in sameness, if you want different results, *you* must do something differently. If you've become a creature of habit, break some of your habits. Drive a different route to work, go to a new restaurant, visit a different church with your neighbors, donate your 1965 Christmas tie to Goodwill, read a book on a new subject. You may find you can break out of predictable patterns and discover new excitement and opportunities.

Are you stuck working in a job you hate? Who's forcing you to get up every morning and go back there? Just like Charlie Brown, you're making your own lunch for the day. If you're tired of bologna, what are you doing to make a different lunch?

Don't you get tired of hearing people looking for excuses for their circumstances? "It's not my fault." "They never trained me for that." "I don't get paid enough to do that." "She shouldn't have pulled out that close in front of me." People are suing because their coffee is too hot, the floors are slippery after a rainstorm, and the road is full of potholes. A man who was fired (after repeated warnings) by IBM for visiting online pornography sites while he was at work sued the company for $5 million, claiming he is an Internet addict who deserves treatment and sympathy rather than dismissal. We hear stories of people planting worms in soup and creating phony car accidents, hoping to find someone to pay for their "misfortunes." Even following "acts of God" (tornadoes, hurricanes, lightning strikes), people look for someone to blame. I don't know of anything more crippling to the ability to see new opportunities than this lack of personal responsibility. If you believe you are being trapped, controlled by your present circumstances, or held back by the government, a spouse, a grandfather, an uncle, your company, or your church, you have already defined your limitations.

I hear about people who drive on bald tires and believe they are under spiritual attack when they have a flat. There are people who failed to study for college entrance exams and then claimed God closed the door. I have seen people show up for a job interview wearing cut-off shorts and a baseball cap, and they went away convinced that the economy was so bad that no one was hiring. And after years of neglecting their marriage, couples conclude it must not have been God's will for them to get married in the first place.

A man may fall many times, but he isn't a failure until he begins to blame someone else.

—Knox Manning

But I Have to Blame Someone!

Shifting personal responsibility has become a national pastime. Blaming, complaining, whining, and procrastination are the immediate results. We see it from the two-year-old to the corporate

CEO. But keep in mind, no individual can achieve worthy goals without accepting accountability for his or her own actions. Accepting responsibility for your life immediately puts you back in the driver's seat. People who look for someone else to blame will always end up feeling like *victims of circumstances*.

Victimism gives your future away.

—Stephen Covey, in *The 8th Habit*

In his book *Every Excuse in the Book,* Craig Boldman offers some excuses for why "It's not my fault!"

- I got severe tire damage on the *Road Less Traveled*.
- I learned the wrong *7 Habits*.
- The *Chicken Soup for My Soul* was contaminated with *E. coli*.
- Someone slipped me some bad affirmations.
- I'm one of those good people bad things happen to.
- There's no evidence of wrongdoing on my part.
- My Inner Child made me do it.[1]

Your Finest Hour

Winston Churchill said, "To every man there comes in his lifetime that special moment when he is figuratively tapped on the shoulder and offered a chance to do a very special thing, unique to him and fitted to his talents. What a tragedy if that moment finds him unprepared or unqualified for the work which would be his finest hour."

Don't expect luck to present you with your finest hour. Remember, luck is when preparation meets opportunity. What three things are you doing right now to prepare for greater opportunity this year—and perhaps to experience your finest hour?

Revolutionary Insight

Just Gimme a Little More Time!

In the first few moments of the movie *Collateral*, the taxi driver, played by Jamie Foxx, tells Tom Cruise's character: "I'm not in this for the long haul. This is just filling in—I'm putting some things together—I'm going to open my own limo service." Cruise asks him, "How long you been doing this?" To which the taxi driver replies, "Twelve years."

This is a classic example of how *life happens*. I once saw a client who had taken a temporary job at a bank. He knew that wasn't where he wanted to be; it was just a fill-in job while he did his real job search. That was fourteen years ago. Life just happened; he got used to where he was and didn't take enough initiative to move on to a higher level of success.

Here is a step-by-step process for change:

1. Clarify your current situation.

    a. I have been in the same job for twelve years with no change in sight.

    b. I detest the monotony of my job.

What opportunities might you have overlooked while waiting for the company to take care of you or for perfect conditions to move in a new direction?

Frequently, a perceived failure or setback actually provides us with an opportunity to take our lives in a new and more fulfilling direction. The portrait artist James Whistler was expected to follow in his military father's footsteps. However, after failing a chemistry test at West Point, he was dismissed from the academy in 1854 for a "deficiency in chemistry." He worked briefly for the Winans Locomotive Works in Baltimore but could not resist his passion for traveling and painting. If not for his ability to turn adversity into opportunity, he might never have created his most famous painting, *Portrait of the Artist's Mother,* commonly known as *Whistler's Mother*. When his scheduled model fell ill and could

2. Seek the advice and opinions of other people. I will ask four or five trusted friends or professionals what they would do if they were in my situation.

3. Identify the alternatives.

   a. I could go back to school and get a degree in education.

   b. I could create a clear focus and do a job search with a company with some advancement potential.

   c. I could start my own chauffeuring service.

   d. I could request a manager's position with my current company.

4. Choose the best alternative. I will start my own chauffeuring service.

5. *Act.* I will create my business plan in the next thirty days, give my two-weeks' notice fifteen days after that, aggressively plan to purchase my own vehicle by that time, and be open for business sixty days from now.

Whether it's choosing a new school, a new place to live, a new car, or a retirement center for a parent, you must keep a clear deadline in view. Otherwise, procrastination will lead to indecision.

not pose, Whistler asked his mother to stand in for the painting, which he did on the back of an old canvas. Despite the fact that she had to sit because of her frailty, Whistler managed to capture her strong Protestant character in her somber pose and expression. It became his most famous painting. This iconic image continues to provide inspiration for artists, cartoonists, and filmmakers, and it has been the focus of three *New Yorker* magazine covers.

The point is this: *Don't wait on perfect conditions for success to happen; just go ahead and do something.* And don't settle for failure—how can you turn a setback into an opportunity?

I see many people blame something outside themselves for their current circumstances and lack of accomplishment. They blame their parents, their teachers, their bosses, their coworkers,

God, or a spouse for those unexpected turns in life. But blaming solves nothing. Instead, it creates fear and hopelessness. It destroys creativity and builds walls that keep other people and potential resources out. Perhaps what you see as an obstacle is God's gentle way of redirecting you to a more fulfilling future. How else can He get your attention? You know that when things are going well we tend to just maintain the status quo. The old adage "The good is the enemy of the great" is true. Sometimes what we see as a disaster is a wake-up opportunity to get back on track.

> The words "It's not my fault" have been symbolically written on the gravestones of unsuccessful people ever since Eve took her first bite of the apple. Until a person takes responsibility for where he is, there is no basis for moving on.
>
> —Andy Andrews, *The Traveler's Gift*

In 1988 I experienced a devastating business loss. Banking and real estate laws seemed to change overnight, and the gentleman's handshake agreements I had on credit lines folded. I was forced to sell a fitness club, culminating in a loss of $430,000 in accumulated profits. With the complications of a forced sale, I also was left with remaining debts of nearly that much again. The IRS was at our front door demanding money that I did not have. Vendors were ready to file suit in a futile attempt to extract payments from my insolvent corporation.

As chairman of the small business development center with our local chamber of commerce, I was embarrassed and humiliated. But I knew I had a choice. I could blame God, the banks, the economy, my partners, or bad luck for this unfortunate turn of events, or I could accept full responsibility for my circumstances and begin to look for positive next steps. Blessed with a supportive wife and friends, I quickly began to explore new directions and opportunities. Yes, I spent time in a dreadful commissioned sales job and struggled to repay those debts for much longer than I ever imagined I would. Yes, I borrowed a car (a 1978 Mercury Zephyr wagon—it used a quart of oil for every hundred miles, the power windows didn't work, and the radio wouldn't play) from a friend to get to those sales appointments. I knew that I was a sitting duck for negative thinking to fill every moment I spent in that old car. I carried a battery-operated cassette player and committed to spend at least two hours each day reading, praying, and listening to positive, uplifting messages of hope and inspiration (a powerful plan I continue today).

I saw in a new light business principles that I had clearly violated. I realized I had leveraged my good reputation into getting credit lines and vendor terms that went beyond what my business could support. I had used payroll deductions as an immediate source of funds to cover daily expenses—rather than paying them directly to the IRS. I discovered countless principles in the book of Proverbs that I had violated with my slick knowledge and ability. I had overlooked what Solomon warned in Proverbs 13:18 (CEV), that "All who refuse correction will be poor and disgraced." I thought persistence was my magic formula, so after seven banks refused to back my plans for purchasing the fitness center I developed a creative plan for making it happen anyway and thus took the investment of three formerly close friends down with me. I ended up experiencing the poverty and shame mentioned by Solomon—plus the loss of three great friendships.

After that I learned new ways of doing business that kept me from being "slave to the lender." The "disaster" allowed me to take a fresh look at who I was, where I was going, and what my strongest areas of competence were.

Today, Joanne and I live in a house that fits a long list of our desired characteristics in the rolling hills just south of Nashville, Tennessee. I have Mondays, Wednesdays, and Fridays blocked out for thinking, writing, and planning. I coach clients one day a week and keep one day free for speaking engagements. The irony is that, if I had continued on the path I was on in 1988, I would certainly not be where I am today. I would have built traditional businesses, hired and managed employees, bought or rented buildings—all tasks I see as emotionally draining. This experience opened my eyes to methods for working independently without having to deal with any of these traditional business issues. The forced redirection allowed me to *see* new opportunities and to improve upon skills I didn't even know I had prior to that "unfortunate event." The success I thought I had then is far surpassed by the peace, sense of true accomplishment, time freedom, and financial income I enjoy today. From my speaking engagements, I create more income in a single day than my hardworking father made from a full year of farm labor.

How many times have you been frustrated or angry at what seemed to be a defeat or failure? Have you ever discovered later on that the failure saved you from a bigger disaster or directed you to something even better? Do you view failure as a disappointment, or do you look for the better opportunity it may be presenting?

From working with people looking for career direction, I have discovered that a job loss or a business failure, while devastating at first, later comes to be viewed by most people as the best thing that ever happened to them. Maury was terminated from his $150,000 a year position with an automotive manufacturer. Although shocked and dismayed, within two weeks he had negotiated an independent contractor position with a competitive company, with more financial opportunity and a much more flexible schedule. In addition, he took advantage of the transition to launch his own vintage car business, a dream that had been dormant for forty-eight years. He explains that the continued success of his previous job would never have given him the opportunity to find this new and higher level of success.

A former humanitarian worker recently wrote to me about being laid off: "I was working sixty hours a week for a local nonprofit. . . . I suddenly realized I had spent nearly five years of my life working for someone else's goals and values—mine were systematically being pushed to the back. . . . With little savings to tide me over, no time to collect contact information (only one hour to clean my desk out while being observed), and at a young age . . . I decided to take the plunge and fly solo. It will be two years in June. I have more work than I could have imagined. . . . Every day, when I lie down to sleep at night, I thank God for being laid off."

Resist the temptation to allow setbacks to fill you with anger and despair. Look for the seeds of opportunity in your situation. Look for the rainbow instead of the storm.

Ninety-nine percent of all failures come from people who have a habit of making excuses.

—George Washington Carver
(chemist who discovered 325 uses for the peanut)

If you are a Revolutionary, if you want to create the life and work of your dreams, then you are going to have to accept 100 percent responsibility for your life. That means giving up all your excuses, all the finger-pointing and blaming, and all the false belief that you are trapped or controlled by your current circumstances. It's challenging at first, I know. But guess what? Just as

POT-SHOTS
Brilliant Thoughts in 17 Words or Less

it has done for me and so many people I've encountered in my work, that acceptance will free up your mind to abilities you may not have even known you had. Before long, opportunities will appear all around you.

Don't expect everyone else to share your belief or enthusiasm. Unfortunately, many of those you encounter, frustrated by their own failures and circumstances, will try to keep you at their level. There will always be an abundance of whiners, naysayers, small thinkers, and dream stealers. You may even find some of your most spiritual friends to be much like Job's friends—who suspected he had sinned to bring on his own woes—and who add to your dismay rather than bringing new hope. Recognize that you are on a different path.

But I Can't Do That!

On May 6, 1954, Roger Bannister ran the first sub-four-minute mile in recorded history. Doctors had said it could not be done—that the human heart would explode with such exertion. Six weeks later an Australian runner duplicated Bannister's feat. Approximately one year later, eight college runners at one NCAA track meet all broke the four-minute mark. What changed? Did humans suddenly evolve to be faster than ever before? Not likely. What did happen is that the level of expectation changed. What had been believed to be impossible was proven to be possible. Most of us operate under clear beliefs about what we are able to accomplish. If those beliefs are changed, the results change as well.

I find many people living their lives within boundaries that exist only in their minds.

—Dan Miller

Motivational speaker Zig Ziglar tells his favorite story about flea training. As he tells it so convincingly, if you put fleas in a jar with a lid on it, they will desperately pop up against the lid in an attempt to escape—for about twenty minutes. Then, once they are fully convinced they can't get out of the jar, you can remove the lid. With a perfectly clear path to freedom, the fleas will remain in the jar and starve to death. They tried to get out once before and they *believe* there is no other option. Who do you know who tried something once—and failed—and now that person is convinced he or she can't do that particular thing?

What artificial barriers have you placed in your life? Are you telling yourself that you are not intelligent enough to finish college, not deserving enough to get a better job, or not creative enough to start your own business? Are you convinced that something is impossible for you or out of your reach? Is it really out of reach, or might it just be beyond your level of belief?

Fears and insecurities become self-fulfilling. "No, I can't do that because I don't have enough talent, money, time, or intelligence." "No, I can't make a difference—things have been this way too long." Unfortunately, no one needs to hold us down if we're down already. As long as we see walls around us or ceilings above us, we're bound to remain limited by them. If you think you can't, you can't. But if you take a fresh look at your abilities, dreams, and passions, you have the potential to break into new arenas of accomplishment that will amaze both you and those around you.

If you don't think you are the best candidate for a new job, do you think the company will convince you that you are? If you don't think you can climb a mountain, do you think you will ever get to the top? No, it never happens that way. If you can't see yourself achieving a new goal, believe me, it will never happen. Ask athletes who win events, and you'll find they believed they could before it really happened.

What does the Bible say about this process? According to

Luke 6:45 (HCSB): "A good man produces good out of the good storeroom of his heart. An evil man produces evil out of the evil storeroom, for his mouth speaks from the overflow of the heart." The thought of a man's heart precedes whatever he says. From our heart come our actions, whether good or evil. And from our thinking comes either success or failure. Believe you're a failure and life will prove you are right. Believe you are trapped and controlled by a bad economy, bad luck, or an unfair government and your experiences will confirm that belief. But expect the good, expect the positive, expect the win, expect the best job, and you'll see God help create that reality in your life.

> Make no small plans;
> they have no magic to stir men's souls.
> —Daniel Burnham

Unfounded fears about your competence and abilities can cripple your unique talents and gifts, which are waiting to be released. Bad job experiences and uninspiring managers can compound those fears. Gloria told me about having been let go from her previous job. The layoff was not a result of incompetence; a part of the company was moving operations overseas. But she tearfully described the intense feelings of rejection she felt, even eighteen months later, and her inability to move forward. Although the inevitable closing of the company was well publicized, her deep pain was obvious as she related the insensitivity of her boss in identifying her last day. He had been belittling her for her entire six-year employment, she explained, so despite the fact that she'd been given plenty of notice and a wonderful severance package, she was still nursing the pain and unable to make new contacts or even dream of a better future.

As we explored her new options, Gloria came to realize she had been not fired but liberated. There's a valuable lesson here:

Revolutionary Insight

You Keep Your F; I'm Keeping My Dream!

When Monty Roberts was in high school, his teacher asked the class to write about what they wanted to do when they grew up. Monty wrote that he wanted to own a ranch and raise Thoroughbred racehorses. His teacher gave him an F and explained that the dream was unrealistic for a boy living in a camper in back of a pickup truck. He would never be able to make this a reality. When the teacher offered the chance to rewrite his paper for a higher grade, Monty told him, "You keep your F; I'm keeping my dream."

Today, Monty's 154-acre ranch in Solvang, California, is home to world-class Thoroughbred racehorses, and his gentle Join-Up method of training horses (and kids) is the inspiration of companies around the world. Join-Up is a method of training horses without the use of pain or force. Monty studied the nonverbal communication between horses and gives a horse the option of accepting the leadership of a human, thus "joining up" rather than being forced into submission.

He and his wife, Pat, have raised their own three children as well as forty-seven foster children, who return regularly to spend time on the ranch. This real-life horse whisperer inspired the book of that title and the Robert Redford movie that propelled Monty to fame and fortune beyond his wildest boyhood dreams. (See http://www.montyroberts.com.)

Now, who's been trying to talk you out of your dream? Who's been telling you you're crazy and it can't be done? What level of success is that person experiencing? Did you ever notice that most naysayers and dream kickers are unhappy and unfulfilled themselves? Don't let them bring you down to their level. Find people who are already performing at the level at which you'd like to be. You will find they will encourage and inspire you even more.

Cry your tears, but remember, resurrection is a daily occurrence. Every morning presents opportunities that were not there the day before. Don't be content with the success of yesterday. Expect new possibilities, even if the circumstances appear to be the same. Of course, it is often difficult to see opportunities when we're stuck in the blur of predictable sameness. That's why endings are so valuable; they force us to take action. Then again, you don't have to wait for the pink slip to change your circumstances.

Are you guilty of limiting your potential because of your narrow thinking? Do you really have only two choices (quit or stay)? Or could you come up with ten alternatives for changing and moving forward? Are you feeling trapped—a victim of the economy, your company, your education, or your financial situation? How will changing your expectations liberate you to see new possibilities you never dreamed of?

> *Man who waits for roast duck to fly into mouth must wait very, very, long time.*
>
> —Chinese proverb

Write Yourself a Check

The comedic actor Jim Carrey grew up in a family so poor that for a time they lived in their Volkswagen van on a relative's lawn. But Carrey believed in his future even when it may have seemed likely he would follow his parents in poverty. From a young age, Carrey knew he had a greater calling; when he was a mere ten years old, he mailed his résumé to *The Carol Burnett Show.* And that sense of hope continued as Carrey got older. The story is told that one night in 1990, when Carrey was a struggling young comic in Los Angeles, he drove his old, beat-up Toyota to the top of a hill. While sitting there, broke, looking down over the city and dreaming of his future, he wrote himself a check for $10 million, put in the notation line "for acting services rendered," and dated it Thanksgiving 1995. He stuck that check in his wallet—and the rest, as they say, is history.

By 1995, Carrey had seen the tremendous success of *Ace Ventura: Pet Detective, The Mask,* and my personal favorite, *Liar Liar.* His per film fee had escalated to $20 million.

Was writing that check just a meaningless trick, or did it really set the stage in some way for his eventual success? When I had the IRS knocking at my door and we were losing our house, I kept a hundred-dollar bill in my wallet. No matter how broke we were, I knew I had that hundred dollars in my pocket. I am convinced that little tactic helped me stay optimistic when everything else seemed hopeless. As a reminder of that, I have freely given that hundred dollars away many times to others who were struggling for hope. What are you doing to direct your thinking toward the future you want?

While I was struggling with the feelings surrounding my own devastating loss several years ago, a friend recommended that I read *Man's Search for Meaning* by Viktor Frankl, the account of the Jewish doctor's experiences as a prisoner during the Holocaust.

Imagine this for a moment: Your family has been taken away. You are stripped of all personal belongings—your home, your possessions, your watch, even your wedding ring are gone. Your head is shaved and your clothes removed, you are marched into a Gestapo courtroom. After you are falsely accused and interrogated, the German high command finds you guilty and sentences you to death or internment in a work camp. These instant decisions were based not on any real evaluation of right or wrong but simply on the appearance of physical health and stamina, or lack thereof. Years of indignity and humiliation follow in the concentration camp. Dr. Frankl watched as most of those "saved" in that initial selection deteriorated physically and still were sent to the gas chambers. No hope. No light at the end of the tunnel. You give up. Right? But wait. Giving up is not the only choice.

Dr. Frankl experienced devastating and terrifying events.

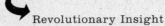

Revolutionary Insight

The Man in the Mirror

Victor Seribriakoff was a "dunce." His teachers believed he had no chance of finishing school, much less finding meaningful employment. So Victor succumbed to the destiny others had prescribed for him. He worked odd jobs here and there, living on the streets with no goal beyond day-to-day survival. Then, at thirty-two years old, Victor took a test that revealed he had an IQ of 161. He was a genius! Victor wondered how that could be, given the life he'd led so far and everything his teachers had told him. Yet he believed the written results. He immediately began writing, inventing, and developing successful business ventures; he was eventually elected chairman of Mensa, a group that requires an IQ of 140 or more.

Behavioral scientists tell us that, by the time we reach the age of two, 50 percent of what we ever believe about ourselves has been formed; by six, 60 percent of our self-belief has been established, and by eight, almost 80 percent. By the time we reach the age of fourteen, over 99 percent of us have a well-developed sense of who and what we believe ourselves to be.

And then there's the bumblebee. Brilliant biologists have determined with precise scientific calculations that bumblebees cannot fly. They have too much body mass for their wingspan. Fortunately, the bumblebees don't believe a word of it! Who do you see in the mirror? A dunce, who lets other people's negative perceptions cloud your sense of self-worth, or a bumblebee, who rises above circumstances and others' expectations? Bring out the genius in yourself by believing in what you really can be!

However, he realized he had the power to choose one thing—his attitude. No matter what the future had in store for him, he could choose his state of mind. Do I throw in the towel or persevere? Do I hate the Gestapo command or forgive them? Do I exist in a world of deprivation and self-pity or endure the hardships?

Dr. Frankl chose to exist in a world he created in his mind. He survived and was finally liberated. His attitude sustained him.

Dr. Frankl further observed that it was not age, education, or even physical health that determined who survived the atrocities of the concentration camps. The only consistent characteristic of those who survived to freedom was *a sense of hope and a constant belief in a better future.* Belief that tomorrow held opportunity and promise. Let me quickly add, this horrendous piece of history certainly saw many individuals, full of hope, who were sent to their deaths regardless. Even hope may not provide an escape in the absence of morality, logic, and reason, a frightening reality we have seen played out more recently in Rwanda and Darfur.

But Dr. Frankl's story remains proof that it is possible to liberate our minds, even in the face of tremendous adversity. We are equipped to rise above negative circumstances to joy, victory, and accomplishment. This, however, is potential, not determinism. You *choose*!! Dr. Frankl lived the belief that life is 10 percent what happens to us and 90 percent how we respond to it. You *choose*!! Remember that happiness is a function of character, not circumstances. All of us can probably think of an instance where we would have been justified to feel like victims of circumstances, but even in the middle of a job loss, personal rejection, or business failure we can choose optimism, joy, and a better future.

If You're a Revolutionary, You Will

- Stop blaming others or thinking circumstances are controlling you.
- Realize you make your own lunch every day.
- Recognize that your obstacle or setback may be an opportunity in disguise.
- Keep your dreams alive—even when others are shooting holes in them.
- Write your own check for your future.

4

DON'T WAIT FOR THE "WIZARD"

If I Only Had a Brain

In the conclusion of the classic movie *The Wizard of Oz*, the beloved characters discovered that the abilities and attributes they'd spent so much time searching for were things they already possessed. Just like Dorothy, the Cowardly Lion, the Tin Man, and the Scarecrow, we don't have to wait for any mysterious wizard to do what we need to do for ourselves.

Too many people are waiting for the wizard in his many forms, including therapist, coach, boss, spouse, and the government, to do what they will ultimately have to do themselves. You'll recall that, in *The Wizard of Oz*, the wizard assigns tasks to the characters that he promises will help them accomplish their goals. His role is much like that of a helpful therapist or coach who recommends actions you can take to overcome an obstacle or achieve a goal. But at the end of the day, no therapist or coach can truly solve your problems, nor can a spouse force you to find work that is meaningful and fulfilling. Similarly, the government is not going to create jobs—*you* create jobs. Your boss may not give you a raise or flexible hours out of the goodness of his or her heart; you need to ask for the things you want.

As soon as you accept responsibility for your own life, you release yourself from the delusion that some miracle is going to make things better. You begin to see another possibility: that only you can bring that miracle into being. You begin to recognize that you are in the driver's seat; you have the ability to follow helpful suggestions from your wizard, but ultimately you must forge your own path. Whether you want a more powerful brain, a heart, courage, a better job, or more money, you need to take steps to make it happen. Remember, no one *owes* you these things—just like no company owes you more money just because you've been there another year. You create more money by creating more value. You find a better job or more fulfilling work by looking inward, making a plan, and taking specific action. Success is not a lottery—and thank goodness for that! The fact is, you can be a winner anytime you want to by recognizing that there is no wizard behind the curtain—only you.

Have you ever noticed that even if God gives you a dream, you are expected to work to make it happen? If you're chosen for the football team, you have to practice and work hard day after day to keep your place. If you're accepted into a prestigious college, you have to study to keep your grades up or the college will ask you to leave. If God calls you to enter the pastorate, you will likely need to invest time and money going to seminary before you will see that dream become reality. It seems that even when dreams are coming true, God requires our part in the process.

This is not bypassing God or stepping ahead of his will. Rather, it is releasing what he has already put inside us. One of the most profound parables in the Bible is the story of the talents. The worker who received five talents realized he was a steward of those talents. He went to work immediately and doubled his gift, returning to the master ten talents. And the master had this to say: "Well done, good and faithful servant! You have been faithful with a few things; I will put you in charge of many things. Come and share your master's happiness!" (Matthew 25:21, NIV).

The worker who received one talent decided he'd just try to hang on to that one talent and hope the master would give him more at some point. But his master replied to him: "You wicked, lazy servant!... Take the talent from him and give it to the one who has the ten talents. For everyone who has will be given more, and he will have an abundance. Whoever does not have, even what he has will be taken from him" (Matthew 25:26-29, NIV).

What do you think our responsibility is for the talents God has given us? Do we take the safe route and tolerate misery and mediocrity in our lives? Or do we step out in faith to maximize the gifts we have been given? I know the words I want to hear when I come face-to-face with the Master.

There is a spiritual life lesson for all of us to gain from seeing how this unfolds. Yes, we can have dreams. And yes, those dreams may come into view. But it requires a clear plan of action, imagination, desire, hard work, self-discipline, and faith. What we have and are today result from God's creation having been shaped and molded by human intelligence and hard work. The ancient Jews recited a prayer every year at Passover that describes how this works:

> Blessed are you, Lord, God of all creation.
> Through your goodness we have this bread to offer,
> which earth has given and human hands have made.
> It will become for us the bread of life.

That prayer reveals a profound spiritual principle: God's gifts are raw materials, not finished products. Think about the most revered sacrament in the church, Holy Communion. Does God give us bread and wine? Where can you find those in nature? You can't. God makes wheat; he doesn't make bread. He makes grapes, not wine. But when we take the raw materials God gives us, we can add our work and give them back to him as an offering.

This is a picture of the spiritual life for each of us. Every one of us has special gifts—singing, mathematical skills, writing, gardening, art, computer skills, selling abilities, teaching others, encouraging others. But whatever our gift is, it's a raw product. It has limited value until we apply the discipline necessary to make it useful to ourselves and others.

Our lives are the bread that we make to offer back to God. We get nothing but raw materials—life doesn't hand us the finished product. Life may even bring us obstacles or heartache along the way. But ultimately our lives are the bread that we prepare. Our lives are what those around us see as the result of what we've done with the raw materials.

You must take responsibility. You cannot change the circumstances, the seasons, or the wind, but you can change yourself.

—Jim Rohn, business philosopher

As the success coach Brian Tracy says, "Your life only gets better when you get better." What are the three things you want to happen this year? What specific steps can you take to move yourself into the growing numbers of the *No More Dreaded Mondays* crowd? Rather than singing with the Scarecrow from *The Wizard of Oz,* "If I only had a brain," recognize what you already have between your own two ears and move forward with confidence, boldness, and enthusiasm.

The tragedy of a man's life is what dies inside of him while he lives.

—Henry David Thoreau

Risk—Danger or Opportunity?

I frequently hear people say they're afraid to apply for a new job, try a new sport, buy a new car, or launch a new business idea because of the *risk* involved. When people are considering a new career or a change of position, they often ask themselves, "Why leave the predictable for the unpredictable? Why take the *risk?*" And yet there is a core issue regarding risk that must be clarified. If you go to Las Vegas and put the deed to your house down on a roll of the dice, that's risky—gambling with no reasonable plan or sense of control. However, if you find yourself in a negative work environment, have checked out your options, and are planning to move to a solid organization with a higher income, how can that be called risk? Risk implies jumping off a cliff with no idea what is at the bottom. It means having no control. In business or career moves, we greatly reduce risk by having a careful plan of action. Call it "seizing an opportunity" rather than "risk." If you are underemployed or undercompensated now and you've clarified your unique gifts and talents and matched those up with a new opportunity, is that *risk*?

In *The Millionaire Mind,* Thomas Stanley examined the characteristics of multimillionaires. All of these people selected an industry for which they have some affinity. It's more than money; it's a feeling of belonging.[1] Once they've found the right industry, they learn more about it, make sure it's a right fit, seek out training, gain experience, and build customer contacts. Stanley concludes, "What is the real risk of starting one's own business under these circumstances?" Perhaps we need a new word for *risk.* It's not a blind leap into the unknown. Rather, it's a calculated move in a clearly defined direction.

In my many years of life coaching high-achieving people, I have observed that they view risk differently from those who fear it. They think it's risky to be trapped in one company; they view security as having the freedom to do what they love on their own terms—the exact opposite of the average person's perception.

Let me make it clear that I am not recommending everyone start his or her own business. But once you have looked at yourself, identified your strongest areas of competence, embraced your dreams and passions, you'll begin viewing your life from a different point of reference. You'll know you are in the driver's seat. You'll no longer be a victim of circumstances. You'll be an independent entity, your own company; you can then choose to have one customer (traditional job) or one hundred in your own venture.

Sometimes the greatest risk is not taking one.

Don't settle for "comfortable misery," a sad state where you're hanging on to what is most predictable and familiar at the risk of letting exciting opportunities pass you by. And don't be like the guy who stopped by the fortune-teller at the local county fair and asked for a glimpse into his future. The fortune-teller looked him over and told him, "You'll be poor, unhappy, and miserable until you're fifty."

"Then what?" asked the man.

"By that time," the fortune-teller said, "you'll be used to it."

When written in Chinese, the word crisis is composed of two characters—one represents danger, and the other represents opportunity.

—John F. Kennedy

Do You Need a Small Fire in Your Life?

Chemists and biologists agree that, when a living system is in a state of equilibrium, it is less responsive to change. Prolonged stagnation can therefore leave a system vulnerable to major disaster. An example in nature would be the absolute prevention of forest fires. Most of us would agree that we want to prevent fires in any way we can. And to keep our parks open to visitors,

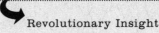

Revolutionary Insight

A Total Waste of Time?

In 1902, an aspiring young writer received a rejection letter from the poetry editor of *The Atlantic Monthly*. Enclosed with a sheaf of poems the twenty-eight-year-old poet had sent was this curt note: "Our magazine has no room for your vigorous verse." The young poet rejected the rejection and went on to see his work published. His name was Robert Frost.

In 1890, a sixteen-year-old found this note from his rhetoric teacher at Harrow, England, attached to his report card: "A conspicuous lack of success." The young man rejected the rejection and went on to become one of the most famous speakers of the twentieth century. His name was Winston Churchill.

We've all heard about Fred Smith's college paper in which he laid out his plan for Federal Express, only to be given a C and told it would never work. The Wright brothers' own father dismissed their ideas about flying as a *total waste of time*. We know that most successful businesspeople go through two to three failures before they develop the idea that really works.

I have seen countless people who had ideas, solutions, and inventions rejected—only to go on to extraordinary success. Have you been turned down for a business proposal? Have you been passed over for a promotion or dismissed in a job interview? Have you been fired? Maybe you need to reject the rejection and go on to achieve real success.

we see a constant emphasis on fire prevention. But fires are a natural part of the cycle of regeneration. A small fire cleans out the area and allows new growth. Preventing even small fires allows a buildup of undergrowth, so that when a fire *does* occur, rather than just cleaning out the ground cover, it destroys even the mature trees. In recent news, we've seen stories of raging fires fueled by years of undergrowth consuming valuable trees, expensive homes, and businesses.

Staying in the same job for twenty years may appear to be a form of security. You may have been complimented on your many years of loyalty and perhaps have received a nice pen or paperweight for staying in the same place. But in fact, you may be a sitting duck for potential disaster.

Is the consistency in your life a blessing, or is it leaving you vulnerable? Have twenty years on the job made you complacent and unaware of the changes that have occurred in the workplace? Do you resist change at all costs?

It's important to allow for flexibility. Trying too hard to keep things constant in our lives can restrict natural growth and positive change, turning any unexpected change into a major disaster. For any system to survive and grow, it must welcome variety. Maybe you need to give up the plaid sport coat and trade in the AMC Pacer. You may need to actually light a little fire in your life today!

POT-SHOTS
Brilliant Thoughts in 17 Words or Less

© ASHLEIGH BRILLIANT 2003. POT-SHOTS NO. 3484.

THEY SAY TOMORROW'S ON ITS WAY ~

BUT NOBODY SEEMS TO KNOW FROM WHICH DIRECTION IT'S COMING.

AshleighBrilliant.com

Thinking Way Outside the Box (and the Bag)

There May Be More Solutions Than What You First See . . .

Many years ago in an Indian village, a farmer had the misfortune of owing a large sum of money to the village moneylender. The old and ugly moneylender fancied the farmer's beautiful daughter, so he proposed a bargain. He would forgive the farmer's debt if he could marry his daughter. Both the farmer and his daughter were horrified by the proposal, but the cunning moneylender suggested that they let providence decide the matter. He told them that he would put a black pebble and a white pebble into an empty money bag. The girl would have to reach in and pick one pebble from the bag. If she picked the black pebble, she would become his wife and her father's debt would be forgiven. If she picked the white pebble, she need not marry him and her father's debt would still be forgiven. If she refused to pick a pebble, her father would be thrown into jail until the debt was paid.

They were standing on a pebble-strewn path in the farmer's field. As they talked, the moneylender bent over to pick up two pebbles. The sharp-eyed girl noticed that he had picked up two black pebbles and put them into the bag. He then asked the girl to pick a pebble. Now, imagine that you were the girl standing in the field. What would you have done? If you had to advise her, what would you have told her?

Careful analysis would produce three possibilities: (1) The girl could refuse to take a pebble—but her father would then be thrown in jail. (2) The girl could pick a black pebble and sacrifice herself in order to save her father from debt and imprisonment. Or (3) The girl could pull out both black pebbles in the bag, expose the moneylender as a cheat, and likely incite his immediate revenge.

Take a moment to think through this story. I've used it with the hope that it will help you see alternate solutions beyond the obvious ones. The girl's dilemma cannot be solved with traditional logical thinking. You may be in a similar situation. You may be in a job you hate—but the pay is great. You have two choices: (1) You can stay in a job you hate. (2) You can leave the job but will then give up the great pay. Are these really all the options? Here is what the girl did.

She put her hand into the money bag and drew out a pebble. Without looking at it, she fumbled and let it fall onto the pebble-strewn path, where it immediately became lost among all the other pebbles. "Oh, how clumsy of me," she said. "But never mind, if you look into the bag for the one that is left, you will be able to tell which pebble I picked." Since the remaining pebble was black, it would have to be assumed that she had picked the white one. And since the moneylender dared not admit his dishonesty, the girl would have changed what seemed an impossible situation into an extremely advantageous one.

Now, how could you see more creative solutions for your situation? A couple of years ago I coached a very successful media executive who came to me with a dilemma. Because he was so respected, he had been given increasing responsibilities over the years. His current position had squeezed out all his family and community commitments. He was working seventy to eighty hours a week, but he had also become used to the $180,000 in annual pay. He was considering whether to just accept his lot in life or to quit his job, give up his salary, and seek a more balanced life. I proposed another choice. Since he was valued, why not approach his superiors with a new solution? Delegate much of his workload to allow him to contribute in his strongest areas of competence. They readily agreed. He was able to go back to a forty-hour workweek; he began playing the cello professionally again, volunteering in his son's school, playing in occasional golf tournaments, and managing his church bookstore. Simply by asking for a less-than-obvious solution, he was able to move into a new season of true success.

Moral of the story: Most complex problems do have a solution, if only we attempt to think beyond the obvious choices.

Breathe Deeply—And Do This . . .

We have a tree in our front yard that was damaged by a storm and ultimately died. A normal person would have cut down the dead tree and removed the stump. But I'm not a normal person. I cringed at the thought of cutting down even a dead tree—and began to look at that tree with different eyes. I called the store where I bought my chain saw and asked if they knew anyone who did wood carvings. Three phone calls later I talked with a lady named Terry. She said that while she did wood carvings in her shop, she had never done anything on a standing tree, but she would be willing to give it a shot. She referenced her website (http://www.carvingsforchrist.com), and we agreed to meet a few days later. After looking at the incredible carvings on her website, I sent her a brief message relaying my excitement about having her come to our house.

I immediately got this message back from Terry:

> NO WAY!!! You're THAT Dan Miller???!?!?!! Well, welcome to the results of my reading your book *48 Days to the Work You Love* (www.48Days.com). What a gas! I was dying in my job, read your book, and realized I really wasn't the bad person "they" were brain washing me into thinking I was. . . . I gave 2 months' notice at my job, and immediately experienced a peace that surpasses all understanding. I started to breathe deeper than I had in years. . . . Life is so good now! I have tons of energy, [am] feeling creative, and can go into my studio and carve away. . . . This has been the best year of my life so far!

Does the life you currently have allow you to breathe deeply? If your breathing is shallow and constrained, why is that? What would it take to release "a peace that surpasses all understanding" for you? Be prepared to take an unusual path. Work that's fulfilling to you may not be immediately seen as practical and realistic by those around you. Trust me, you will not find "tree carver" in the U.S. Labor Department's *Dictionary of Occupational Titles*.

Terry did come out to our house. She was able to *see* two amazing faces in that dead tree. We think the faces look perhaps like Abraham and Moses. Instead of an ugly stump, we now have a permanent piece of art in our yard. We have added flowers and shrubs in our little "wisdom garden," and it's the first place for conversation when people visit our home. Make sure you are doing work that touches your soul and releases a peace not experienced by those trapped in meaningless jobs.

The more I work with people searching for meaningful work, the more I realize this is not just a search for current "best trends" in employment—or for a reasonable paycheck, or even for applying for the highest academic degree you may have. *This is a process of releasing that unique genius, purpose, mission, or calling that only you have been placed on earth to fulfill. Don't ignore that task.* Don't compromise what you have the ability and the passion to do. Be relentless in your pursuit—clarify the "what," and the "how to" will begin to appear.

See the Opportunity

While registering his car in Miami, Louie Di Raimondo spotted a hot dog vendor and bought a dog. Then he saw a *For Sale* sign hanging on the cart. On impulse, he bought it for fifteen hundred dollars and set up his own business. But in his hurry to get up and running, Di Raimondo forgot to remove the *For Sale* sign. The first day, he sold more than one hundred hot dogs, but what intrigued him the most was the number of people asking if they could buy his cart.

Today, Di Raimondo sells more than four thousand carts a year out of a Miami showroom. He now has flower carts, pretzel carts, and coffee carts in addition to the original hot dog stands and generates more than $30 million annually in company sales.[2]

Sometimes the opportunity is right in front of us—if we have our eyes open. This is the kind of seeing that is required to join the ranks of those who are experiencing *No More Dreaded Mondays*. It's not necessary to be an inventor, a Ph.D., a mathematical whiz, or an intellectual genius, but you do need to be willing to see things that others may not. And yes, you can train yourself to recognize this kind of opportunity.

No Shoes—Send Shoes

In the spring of last year, I talked with two gentlemen, both in the landscaping business. The first complained bitterly about customers who were hard to please, did not pay their bills on time, and didn't understand the big picture of landscaping. He went on to say that his machines would break down through no fault of his own and that he was filing for bankruptcy that day.

The next morning I spoke with the man who takes care of my own landscaping and lawn maintenance. He told me how great business was, how he had just raised prices 10 percent without losing any business, and how much he enjoyed his customers. He went on to tell me that a customer had offered to build him a new building for his equipment in exchange for ongoing landscaping work. He asked me my advice about building four apartments on the second floor of his new building to rent to his own workers as another source of income. He has recently added concrete fountains and stone patios to his list of offerings in response to multiple customer requests.

Both of these business owners are in the same business, in the same town, experience the same seasonal changes, and have access to exactly the same resources.

This reminds me of the story of two shoe salesmen traveling to a foreign country to sell shoes. The first salesman called immediately and said, "Get me the next flight home. No one here wears shoes." The second salesman called back and said, "Send me our entire inventory. No one here wears shoes!"

Remember the often quoted proverb "As a man thinketh in

his heart, so is he." If you think you are trapped, you are. If you think you don't have enough education, you don't. If you think you'll never get ahead, you won't.

Obviously, the counterpart to that is that if you think the world is full of great options, it is. If you think you have some excellent skills to offer a company or in your own business, you do. If you can see yourself doubling your income over the next three years, it's likely to happen.

What could you do to find a more authentic fit in your work? Could you restructure your workweek, recognizing the company needs forty hours of productive contribution but perhaps you could be there for four ten-hour days and have three days off each week? Or, as many nurses do now, perhaps you could work three twelve-hour shifts and still be paid for a full forty-hour week. Could you work from home for twenty hours, or be paid for your results rather than your time? Could you formalize that dormant dream into a profitable use of your time?

Janusian Thinking

In Greek mythology, the god Janus has two faces looking in opposite directions—a symbol of the concept that any situation can be viewed in opposite ways. You could work more hours to be more successful, or you could work fewer. You could grow your business, or you could make it smaller. While working more and growing your business seem logical formulas for success, what about the other options? Years ago I coached an overworked printer. We looked at the past records of his business. In the preceding eight years, his business had grown by nearly 50 percent each year; however, his profits had stagnated. We segmented his business into five areas of revenue production. My suggestion, which he implemented, was to eliminate three of those areas. Yes, he reduced revenues dramatically, but he also eliminated seven employees, expensive equipment, and eighty-hour weeks—and immediately increased his monthly profits.

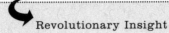

Revolutionary Insight

I'm Not Looking for a Handout; I'm Looking for . . .

Fifty-four-year-old Jackie was released from prison in February 2003 with a history of drug problems and nothing but the clothes on her back. Shortly afterward, she was fortunate enough to be invited to a women's luncheon where she met my wife. She left with a gift of four hundred dollars to purchase a sewing machine.

Today she has six sewing machines and a thriving business. Working out of her own apartment, Jackie has developed a reputation for quality tailor-made clothes and beautiful draperies and upholstery accents. I am helping her shape her business with proper pricing, marketing, and time management. She was recently reunited with her family and enjoys her role as a loving grandma. Jackie appeared with me on a TV station here in Nashville as an example of someone who started with all the odds against her and rose to a full and meaningful life.

Jackie could have used all the excuses I commonly hear. She was too old, too uneducated, and too poor. She could have cried discrimination because she's African American and on parole with a prison record. But this was her statement to me the first time we met. She said, "Dan, I'm not looking for a handout; I'm looking for an opportunity." What a refreshing frame of reference. Rather than expecting the welfare system, the church, luck, or her family to *rescue* her, she sought out her own unique *opportunities.* Here is a woman who has the mind-set to reject failure and to take personal responsibility for her present condition and the future she deserves.

What are you doing that seems logical and reasonable enough but may in fact be limiting your success? In this age of "bigger is better," what could you do to defy the prevailing logic? Experiment with Janusian thinking in some area of your life today. Going with the crowd may not be in your best interests. Remember, even a dead fish will appear to be making progress as long as it's going along with the current. Sometimes it's easy to assume that what is most popular is also the best. But seldom is that true. McDonald's hamburgers and Ford cars are very popular, but few people would argue that they are the best in their field. The great majority of people never enjoy the best of anything simply because they don't look for it or expect it. Learn to question what is most popular and look for the very best in your work choices. As Paul said in the twelfth chapter of Romans: "And do not be conformed to this world: but be ye transformed by the renewing of your mind, that ye may prove what is that good, and acceptable, and perfect will of God" (12:2).

Toward the end of his life, George Bernard Shaw was asked what person in history he would most like to have been. His response was that he would most like to have been the George Bernard Shaw he might have been and never became.

When you begin to see beyond the traditional job model, your mind will begin to open up to creative ways of work that may not have much in common with the old nine-to-five model. Even much of the standard business information may not apply to what you are trying to do. You may not need to rent a building, get a bank loan, buy inventory, or obtain a sign permit. Michael Dell (Dell computers), Pierre Omidyar (eBay), Larry Page and Sergey Brin (Google), Chad Hurley and Steve Chen (YouTube), and Mark Zuckerberg (Facebook) did not follow standard business methods in building their companies. Traditional business plans and principles often don't work for today's freelancers—home-based businesspeople, craftsmen, artists, writers, consultants, and contract workers—whose numbers are exploding.

If It Ain't Broke, Break It!
Familiarity May Be Keeping You from Progressing
Toward a Better Life

While the statement in this section heading may violate your sense of proper English grammar, it embraces what we know about today's work environment. Doing things the way they were done twenty years ago is very dangerous. As a matter of fact, Peter Drucker, the late brilliant business thinker, said that if you are doing things the same way as you were even one year ago, you are probably being left behind. Such is the speed of change in the workplace today.

Here are some statements I have heard from clients recently:

- "I've wasted many years of my life."
- "I got too comfortable."
- "I'm suffering from burnout."
- "I feel like I'm a box of parts and nothing fits together."
- "I feel like a prostitute—in return for a very nice salary, they've taken my heart, soul, and mind."
- "My job has ruled my life."
- "I've been too complacent."
- "I'm on a greased slide to Purgatory."
- "I feel like I'm stuck in *Groundhog Day*."

An example of how dangerous it is to stick to conventional wisdom when the world is changing involves the dramatic transformation of the game of football in 1906. Before that year, football had been a low-scoring game of running and kicking. Guys in leather helmets plodded down the field with the "three yards and a cloud of dust" strategy that was common to every team. Then the forward pass was legalized, making it possible to gain forty yards with one throw. During that first season, however, most teams stayed with the tried-and-true way of playing the game.

One team took another approach. St. Louis University's coaches adapted to this new option and switched to an offense that used the forward pass extensively. That first season they outscored their opponents 402 to 11!

*Everyone is born a genius, but the process of living
degeniuses them.*
—Buckminster Fuller

Seek out ways to bring new methods to your work. You may
want to take some courses to keep you at the top of your field.
You may want to explore completely new fields. You may see a
new opportunity in elder care, telecommunications, mediation,
arts and drama, or alternative medicine. Find something in your
life today that ain't broke and break it! Look for ways to experiment with break-it thinking.

*Get excited and enthusiastic about your own dream. This
excitement is like a forest fire—you can smell it, taste it,
and see it from a mile away.*
—Denis Waitley

I have spent a lot of years in academic environments where
the only things valued are those that can be quantified and meas-
ured. In fact, there are many personal strengths that won't get
you an A in college but may open doors for opportunity and service. How do you measure a person's ability to love or understand
or encourage another? Similarly, there are ways to fulfill your
purpose and calling that may not fit neatly in a traditional process
of measuring intelligence. As I have seen people emerge successfully from inevitable life transitions, I have become convinced
that authentic intelligence means having the courage to find the
environment where your God-given passions and talents can
bloom and thrive.

No one has to wait for a sudden burst of intelligence, a bolt of lightning, or a mystical experience. While any of us would welcome a direct supernatural message from God to get us started on the path to success, it is not necessary. With what you have and where you are, you can begin the process of finding productive, meaningful, and profitable work.

> *Parties who want milk should not seat themselves on a stool in the middle of a field in hopes that the cow will back up to them.*
>
> —Elbert Hubbard

If You're a Revolutionary, You Will

- See opportunities where others see obstacles.
- Recognize that every change cracks open the door for another opportunity.
- Look for the best, not the most popular.
- Accept full responsibility for your results, rather than expect to be compensated for time alone.
- Enjoy making the "bread" that represents your life.
- See the future with optimism, hope, boldness, enthusiasm, and the confidence that can come only from having faith in what may not yet be reality.

5

DONALD'S NOT COMING—
FIRE YOURSELF!

Fire Yourself . . .

In the last chapter, I urged you to change your perspective on set-backs and obstacles in order to *see* opportunities where others see failure. In this chapter, I ask you to stretch your thinking in the hope that you'll recognize possibilities you have not noticed in the past.

So here are some questions to help you stretch your thinking. What would you do if you got fired today? Would you panic, complain to your loved ones, and go whine with all the others who are also out of a job? Would you contact the bank and tell them you probably won't be able to make the mortgage payment next month? Would you cancel your golf membership to save the monthly fee? Would you pull your kids out of that great private school? Would you run down to Home Depot and apply for a ten-dollar-an-hour job there?

These are all actual responses I've seen from competent peo-ple who have gotten that news. The typical response to the loss of a job is to immediately begin expecting less—to assume that any unwelcome change will force a downsizing of income, time, and freedom. Why is that such a common first response? Why is it not just as likely that, when presented with this kind of change, you can actually *increase* your income, fulfillment, and standard of living?

In response to one of my articles that called for a healthier approach to money, I got this message from a reader: "The thought that I have had for years is 'I just want enough money to get by.' In turn, that is all I ever had."

Ah yes, "As a man thinketh in his heart, so is he."

Katie was laid off from her corporate job when she was five months pregnant. While initially shocked and distraught, she now sees that event as a blessing in disguise. The six months' severance pay she received gave her time to see her opportunities with new eyes. Katie says, "I knew the long hours were incompatible with the kind of mother I wanted to be." About the same time, her husband's local professional association, the American Society of Landscape Architects, needed an executive director but could not afford to hire one full-time. Katie sent them a proposal for the duties she could fulfill, and they accepted it immediately. Soon thereafter, a sister organization asked if she could provide the same services for them. She now serves as executive director for these two nonprofit organizations and still has more time for her family than ever before. She gets VIP treatment at hotels and restaurants as a meeting planner, receives all pertinent mail at her home, has very flexible hours, and experiences a great sense of service and being connected. But, you might think, she must have taken a pay cut to have so much free time and enjoy so many perks. Actually, her pay works out to be about twenty-eight dollars an hour, significantly more than in her corporate position.

We don't see things as they are; we see things as we are.

—Anaïs Nin

Those who are living in the land of *No More Dreaded Mondays* see opportunities where others see roadblocks.

"You Ain't Goin' Nowhere, Son"

Name just about any successful businessperson, politician, entertainer, or innovator, and it's likely his or her road to success was paved with failure, firings, and people saying that he'll never make it, that she's crazy, or that what he's trying to achieve is impossible. You may have heard the story of how Walt Disney arrived in Los Angeles with forty dollars in his pocket and experienced bankruptcy multiple times before Mickey Mouse arrived to save the day. Mr. Disney and never-say-die entrepreneurs like him recognize that three steps forward and two steps back still have a net result of one step of progress. Michael Bloomberg (mayor of New York City), Larry King (talk show host), Bernie Marcus (Home Depot founder), and Jesse Ventura (former governor of Minnesota) all got fired along the way to their ultimate successes. Research indicates that, if you are under thirty, the likelihood you will be fired in the next twenty years is 90 percent. If you can decide to see your own "failures" as necessary parts of your progress, you will separate yourself from the average person and put yourself on the same track as the next Bill Gates, Sam Walton, or Thomas Edison.

> *A man of character finds a special attractiveness in difficulty, since it is only by coming to grips with difficulty that he can realize his potentialities.*
>
> —Charles de Gaulle

Charlie Brown discovered an important lesson about failure after building a beautiful sand castle. As soon as he stood back to admire his masterpiece, it got flattened by a huge wave. Staring at the now smooth spot where his day's work had been moments before, he pondered aloud, "There must be a lesson here

Recognize These Famous Failures?

• The first time Jerry Seinfeld walked onstage as a professional comic, he looked out at the audience, froze, and totally forgot how to talk. He stumbled through a minute and a half of material and was booed off the stage.

• Winston Churchill failed the sixth grade.

• Steven Spielberg dropped in and out of Saratoga High School in Saratoga, California, finally graduating in 1965 from what he called the "worst experience" of his life and "hell on Earth." He applied to attend film school at UCLA and at USC three times but was unsuccessful due to his C grade average. After Spielberg became famous, USC awarded him an honorary degree, and in 1996 he became a trustee of the university.

• In 1954 the manager of the Grand Ole Opry fired Elvis Presley after one performance. He told Presley, "You ain't goin' nowhere, son. You ought to go back to drivin' a truck."

somewhere, but I don't know what it is." You may have had a similar experience. But rather than deciding never to build another castle, I trust you simply realized that building a castle so close to the crashing waves is not a good idea. A castle moved back fifty feet and surrounded by rocks will have a much longer life span.

Learn from any failure. See it as a stepping stone toward the success you ultimately want. Don't accuse God of blocking you. "Consider it a great joy, my brothers, whenever you experience various trials, knowing that the testing of your faith produces endurance. But endurance must do its complete work, so that you may be mature and complete, lacking nothing" (James 1:2-4 (HCSB). Are you ready to take the wisdom from your "failures" and turn it into accelerated future success?

Years ago I was in the used car business in Southern California. I used to pride myself on making money on every single car I purchased. But an older gentleman named Cecil, who worked for me wiping the cars down each morning and talking to customers if I was busy, gently told me that if I was making money on every car, then I was missing a lot of opportunity and playing it far too safe. By risking failure (loss of money on a given car), I would open myself up to many more deals and, over the course of a year, make far more money. His advice proved to be invaluable and dramatically increased my total business.

Tap Your Creativity

Thomas Edison had an intriguing way of tapping into the mixture of thoughts and dreams we all have in those moments just before we fall asleep—a highly creative state of mind. Daniel Goleman, Paul Kaufman, and Michael Ray, the authors of *The Creative Spirit*, explain his method: "He would doze off in a chair with his arms and hands draped over the arm rests. In each hand he held a ball bearing. Below each hand on the floor were two pie plates. When he drifted into the state between waking and sleeping, his hands would naturally relax and the ball bearings would drop on the plates. Awakened by the noise, Edison would immediately make notes on any ideas that had come to him."[1]

What are you doing to tap into your creative ideas? For years I have kept a writing pad next to my side of the bed. I grab the pad at various times during the night to jot down ideas that appear when I'm in a more relaxed state of mind. Those ideas have been the seeds for nearly every project I have completed. What idea is hanging out just below your day-to-day conscious thinking? I fear that our busy lives and the urgency of our pace may crowd out even God's quiet voice. Look for ways to hear that voice. What could you develop, write, distribute, broker, or offer as a service to release a new level of success?

We've all heard the statement "Life happens." As blunt as it sounds, there is a lot of truth in that statement. High school blows by; college is a blur; marriage, kids, and mortgages seem to appear almost overnight; and one job leads into the next. Before you know it, you're planning for retirement and wondering, How did I get here?

Of course you know the frog-in-the-kettle story. Whether the story is true or not, the principle is a worthy one. If you throw a frog in a pan of hot water, he'll immediately jump out. But if you put that frog in a pan of lukewarm water, you can slowly turn up the heat and that poor frog will cook to death without moving an inch. The changes are so slow and subtle that he never feels the need to respond.

I hear lots of fascinating stories from people who sound like that poor frog. Here's part of a recent letter from a reader describing his work situation:

> I work as a rural letter carrier. . . . I have been at the same job, in the same Post Office, in the same town for twenty years. I hate the job! Have hated it for fifteen years or so. Have hated it with a passion since my second son was born. It steals my life. I've stood it as long as I can. If I don't get out I'll drown or explode.

Well, at least he recognizes he's in hot water! But with all the opportunities available today, why would someone spend fifteen years in a job after realizing he hated the position? How does a person spend forty to fifty hours a week doing something he or she detests? Maybe I'm just impatient, but if I find myself in hot water, I start looking for an escape in about fifteen minutes, not fifteen years. The interesting thing in many situations like this is that the person eventually gets fired. (He or she usually sets subtle events in motion to ensure this.) The person frequently becomes discouraged, may lower his or her expectations, and just settles in for that comfortable but predictable misery. But then the firing comes anyway. And then he or she immediately begins

Revolutionary Insight
I Don't Hate My Job, but . . .

When I met Mike Sparks, he was working at Nissan manufacturing, in a job that most people would consider the American dream. Great pay, great benefits, and all the security of a traditional job. But he was restless, looking for more.

Mike says I'm the only one who encouraged him to explore some new options and take action. When we first met, he was already experimenting with selling cars on eBay. In one of his initial transactions, Mike bought a red Jaguar convertible, checked every detail, sold it online, and made more money from the car's sale than he would have made in a month at his "real" job. After looking at the success he had already experienced, I encouraged him to quit his job and expand his car business to a full-time opportunity.

Everyone else told him he was crazy for thinking about leaving a great job. But last year Mike sold 150 cars from his MidTN Autos (http://www.midtnautos.com) in Smyrna, Tennessee. There are approximately 135 car dealers in the same county as Mike, but fully 60 percent of his sales last year were completed over the Internet. He's delivered cars to Costa Rica, Germany, and a whole lot of other interesting places.

In looking at any business idea, I encourage the owner to have what I call a *unique selling proposition* (USP). What will you be doing that is not being done well by anyone else? Mike's USP was that he was one of the first to perfect the process of selling cars on the Internet.

I have purchased eight vehicles from Mike and his wife, Felicia, in the last couple of years. Here's yet another example of someone who looked inward, recognized his unique strengths, created a plan, and acted on that plan.

to see all kinds of possibilities for better options. But it shouldn't take a pink slip to get us out of the boiling pot. Why is our vision so clouded by the status quo? Why is the good the enemy of the best? Why does it take getting fired to force someone to take the initiative in finding better choices?

Hire Yourself

Here is my suggestion for how to get yourself in the right mind-set to stretch your thinking. Why don't you fire yourself today? Now I'm not even suggesting that you really change anything. Don't quit your job. Just *imagine* that you were not working anywhere. Then tonight ask yourself, Why would I *hire* myself? And answer the following questions:

- What are my highest areas of competence?
- How do those translate into marketable skills?
- What companies, organizations, or industries would welcome those skills? What kind of business could I create to capitalize on those skills?
- Knowing what I know now, do I want to work for the same company tomorrow? If so, I recognize it's a good fit; I'm grateful for it and will make my finest contribution there.
- If not, how can I create a plan to begin a better life?

Don't wait until the water boils. Get out of that hot water today. Yes, there really are plenty of ponds with cool, clear, refreshing water just waiting for you.

Adopt the Tigger Factor

Would you like to learn a simple technique for seeing things in new ways and stretching your thinking? A short reframing exercise may help. My academic background is in clinical psychology, but I've always wondered why so many psychologists focus exclu-

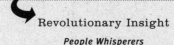

Revolutionary Insight

People Whisperers

In Chapter 3, I wrote about the real-life horse whisperer who inspired the 1995 book and the 1998 movie of the same name. In the movie, Robert Redford played the man who knew that violence is never the answer when attempting to calm wild horses. Well, that same principle is growing in popularity outside horse-training circles. Today it is being applied successfully by corporations, government agencies, school administrators, and people who work with at-risk youth, violent offenders, and many others.

Thanks to a consistent set of principles, communication, and trust, people whisperers can defuse tension and potential conflict. *The Future* magazine identifies "people whispering" as one of the highest-paying careers of the next twenty years and defines its practitioners as those who "are particularly skilled at calming the most irate customers and building relationships with key clients."

This is an example of a new opportunity that makes use of skills that formerly might have been best utilized in poorly paid traditional jobs. If you have been trained as a counselor, schoolteacher, or mediator, you may find a great opportunity as a people whisperer.

sively on pathology and dysfunction. What about the positive side, the moments when human beings are at their absolute best? It seems we can give everyone a label, categorizing every action as a dysfunction of some kind. My wife would likely be labeled an enabler because she enjoys helping people. I've been accused of being in denial because I choose to focus on the good in my past rather than the bad. My son was deemed to have attention deficit/hyperactivity disorder (ADHD) because he found it hard to sit still in a traditional classroom. Now he's executive director of an organization in Rwanda. Some of my best friends have been prescribed Prozac to calm their rapid flows of ideas. Now certainly there are real psychological dysfunctions that need to be diagnosed and treated. But I fear our society is way too quick to diagnose diseases that need to be treated. What if we were just as quick to champion the uniqueness and creativity that children and adults display rather than categorizing anything unusual as a dysfunction?

I like to utilize what I call the "Tigger Factor." You probably remember Tigger from the Winnie-the-Pooh stories as the over-enthusiastic, "can-do," optimistic friend of everyone in the stories. And then there was Eeyore. You know: Eeyore the donkey. Shy, withdrawn, lonely, and terminally depressed. Precisely the sort of personality who, upon being fired, would acknowledge that he'd known it was coming all along. Eeyore is typically suspicious, fearful that people are trying to do him harm. With that kind of thinking, a person will see limitations, not possibilities. I choose to believe that everyone is out to bring me happiness and help me reach my goals. And I try to do the same for them. Having a positive attitude does not mean that problems and frustrations disappear. But I'm confident that the Tigger Factor helps me find solutions much faster than I would if I went the way of the donkey. I believe the world is plotting to do me good!

If you'd like to join me in combating the Eeyore Factor, here are some tips:

1. WHEN OBSTACLES APPEAR, don't assume "everyone hates me." Rather, see these challenges as opportunities to grow and succeed in new ways. Without challenges, you will never improve.

2. REMEMBER A TIME in your life when a seeming disaster opened the door to something good.

3. IF YOU LOSE YOUR JOB, expect that now you'll find your dream job with better pay.

4. STOP THINKING OF your morning wake-up call as an alarm clock. Start reaching for what the motivational speaker Zig Ziglar calls the "opportunity clock"!

I've always been the opposite of a paranoid. I operate as if everyone is part of a plot to enhance my well-being.

—Stan Dale

Think about the many things you encounter each day that may present opportunities for a solution that would be the seed for your big idea.

• If there is no good reading in the waiting room, what could you supply? I know a gentleman who does just that. He supplies great magazines to local waiting rooms that are covered by advertisements promoting local businesses. In doing so, he has netted over $500,000 annually for many years.

• If your back hurts at the office, could you develop a better ergonomic chair design that will make you a millionaire?

• If the coffee is atrocious in the break room, what are five solutions you could create that would make you a hero with workers everywhere and put money in your bank account?

• If people complain about parking at the airport and having to catch a bus to the terminal, could you create a shuttle service from your front door, the way Jeff and Paul did with Shuttle-MAX? (See http://www.shuttlemax.net.)

• If you see nothing but sugary soft drinks at your health club, could you offer to install healthy snacks and drinks, the way I did in a large fitness center several years ago, and generate a significant monthly income?

• What humorous gadget could you create to break the boredom for people staring at their computer screens all day long?

Just keep your eyes and ears open, and you'll begin to see opportunities in any challenge or irritation that people encounter daily.

Unleash Your Creativity

A recent study conducted by Sony Ericsson shed some light on where our best ideas are generated.[2] Here's something to think about: Eighty-one percent of us have our best ideas *outside* the office. Top times for idea generation: while we're in the car, while we're in bed, and while we're socializing. Surprisingly, at the bottom of the list was the pub or local watering hole.

Whatever you do, don't forget to write your ideas down—and then *act* on them. As Steven Spielberg once warned, "Good ideas are only given to you for a limited amount of time. If you don't act on them, they belong to someone else."

Maybe Not!

The next time you come up with an idea that others are finding hard to embrace, remember these quotations:

Well informed people know it is impossible to transmit the voice over wires and that were it possible to do so, the thing would be of no practical value.

—Editorial in the *Boston Post*, 1865

While theoretically and technically television may be feasible, commercially and financially I consider it an impossibility, a development of which we need waste little time dreaming.

—Lee de Forest, quoted in the *New York Times*, 1926

There is no reason for any individual to have a computer in their home.

—Ken Olsen, president of Digital Equipment Corporation,
at the Convention of the World Future Society, 1977

The ordinary "horseless carriage" is at present a luxury for the wealthy; and although its price will probably fall in the future, it will never, of course, come into as common use as the bicycle.

—*Literary Digest*, October 14, 1899

I'm just glad it'll be Clark Gable who's falling on his face and not Gary Cooper.

—Gary Cooper on his decision not to take the leading role in *Gone with the Wind*

Human Filing Cabinets?

I ran across the term *human filing cabinets* recently in reference to office buildings—and it made my skin crawl. Much has been said about the depersonalization of the modern technology worker's work space. How can one be creative, innovative, and contributing when working in an environment that has all the ambience of a veal-fattening pen? When I drive by the high-rise buildings in my area (I consider anything where you can't have your feet in the grass in thirty paces a high-rise), I cringe to think about all those people trapped inside surroundings they endure to survive. Yes, I've visited enormous corporate facilities with natural lighting, beautiful artwork, lovely plants, and music playing softly, but it's a challenge to get beyond the demoralizing impact of most high-rise office spaces.

Clearly, I'm not the only one who thinks this way. Here's a piece from *The Dilbert Principle,* by Scott Adams:

Boss: We've got a lot of empty cubicles because of downsizing. I hired the Dogbert construction company to convert part of the office into prison cells which we'll lease to the state.

Dilbert: **Sounds like a big job.**

Boss: Nah, a little paint, new carpet and we're there.

Later in the cartoon, we learn that the plan to use spare cubicles as prison cells had to be abandoned because of too many complaints . . . from the prisoners!

Distributed Workers

The good news is, the cell-like cubicles Dilbert describes have taken a big hit in the last couple of years. Latest figures from the Bureau of Labor Statistics show that America has 28.7 million telecommuters, or "distributed workers"—those people who work for traditional companies but aren't confined to traditional offices. That number is up from 10.9 million in 2000. Thirty percent of managers and professionals now work at home at least part of the time. Forgoing everything from long commutes to office politics, these Revolutionaries may work on their back deck, from the local Starbucks, or on the beach in Acapulco.

Best Buy is one of the hottest companies to embrace this new work model. Its new "results-only work environment" (ROWE) seeks to demolish decades-old business expectations that equate physical presence with productivity. The goal at Best Buy is to judge performance on output instead of hours.

So now workers pulling into the company's headquarters at 2:00 P.M. aren't considered late. Nor are those pulling out at 2:00 P.M. seen as leaving early. There are no schedules. No mandatory meetings. Work is no longer a place where you go but something you do. It's okay to take conference calls while you hunt, collaborate from your lakeside cabin, or log on after dinner so you can spend the afternoon with your four-year-old.

There has been a subtle shift going on for several years, but Best Buy is the most open about the new work flexibility. At IBM, 40 percent of the workforce has no official office; at AT&T,

a third of managers can work from anywhere they choose. Sun Microsystems calculates that it's saved $400 million over six years in real estate costs by allowing nearly half of all employees to work anywhere they want. And this trend seems to have legs. A recent Boston Consulting Group study found that 85 percent of executives expect a big rise in the number of unleashed workers over the next five years. In fact, at many companies the most innovative new product may be the structure of the workplace itself.[3]

So how about you? Would you thrive in a work environment where your value was judged solely on the results you produced? Would you welcome the freedom to show up at 2:00 P.M. on Monday and to take Thursday afternoon to go fishing? And yes, I realize that some jobs are necessarily time-connected. But I suspect that about 80 percent of what we have as jobs could work with this model.

Here are some of the reasons why *everyone* benefits from a distributed worker model:

• Companies can save significantly on fixed costs, such as rent and utilities.

• Expensive multiple-story corporate offices may not even be necessary.

• Studies show that distributed workers are *more* productive, not less, as many companies used to suspect.

• Such workers are not wasting their time on nasty commutes, unproductive committee meetings, watercooler chats, or flying paper airplanes to the cute new gal in accounting.

• Cutting out that unproductive time means faster, more focused results.

• Once you pull people away from mind-numbing office protocol, the brightest and best devote their time and energy to increasing the company's creativity, innovation, and competitive advantage.

POT-SHOTS
Brilliant Thoughts in 17 Words or Less

• Distributed workers may have dedicated work spaces available in their communities but not have to make the trip to the office.

• Distributed workers can live where they want—by the ocean, in the mountains, in the city, or in the country, all while working for the same company. Individual lifestyle choices are encouraged; even while contributing to the company goals, distributed workers can "have a life."

Whether you are the employer or the employee, you can benefit from these possibilities. In fact, both companies and individuals had better be open to this option if they want to stay on the leading edge of innovation. Otherwise, they risk losing out to companies like Best Buy and IBM, which are already seeing the direct effect this new way of working is having on their bottom lines, and the happiness of their workers. Those high-rise office buildings can be leased to the government for prison cells or to farmers for veal-fattening pens.

If we are hoping to produce more creative products or offer innovative services and solutions, then we cannot treat our most important resource—our people—like simple machines. Offices that resemble human filing cabinets will ultimately suck the life, energy, and intelligence out of even the brightest and most creative souls. Too much of the current corporate environment stifles rather than enhances creativity and innovative thinking. Look for environments that will stimulate your thinking, not block it. Notice when you are most creative and seek out a work space, whether in a traditional office or outside one, that re-creates that environment. As an employer, you should be able to recognize a working environment that drains rather than enhances worker productivity.

You *can* increase your creativity. The process is just like exercising yourself into better physical health. Here are a few techniques to transform your current work environment into a more creative zone:

- Go for a long walk.
- Sit quietly for twenty minutes.
- Think one "impossible" thought every day.
- Remove "Yes, but" from your vocabulary.
- Say to yourself, "I can do this!"
- Form a creativity support group.

If you make these exercises part of your daily routine, you'll be amazed at how much they will help you stretch your thinking.

Life is either a daring adventure, or nothing. Security does not exist in nature, nor do the children of men as a whole experience it. Avoiding danger is no safer in the long run than exposure.

—Helen Adams Keller

Is Your QWERTY Holding You Back?

Do you know what qwerty is? Unsure? Then just glance down at your computer keyboard. The first six letters at the top left spell it out—QWERTY. Do you know that these letters were arranged that way to make the job of typing more *difficult*? The first commercial typewriter, developed by Christopher Latham Sholes in 1873, originally had keys that were arranged alphabetically. However, a problem soon arose. People became so adept at using the keyboard that the typewriter keys would jam when struck in quick succession. In order to overcome this problem, Sholes decided to make typing as slow as he could. He placed the most frequently used keys as far from one another as he could. His keyboard became known as the QWERTY keyboard.

Today, every aspect of your computer is designed for maximum speed and efficiency—you simply cannot outtype the speed your keyboard is capable of handling. But we continue to use a speed trap—a keyboard design that's over 130 years old. The only reason: we have become accustomed to having things in a certain way and are very resistant to change.

This is a classic example of maintaining the status quo—doing things the way they've always been done—without asking, "Why are we doing this?" I see people sending out one hundred résumés, then sitting back and waiting for job offers—that's an old, ineffective model. People who are looking for the job with "security and predictability," guaranteed benefits, and retirement plans are following an old model that is diminishing rapidly. We're not going to see it again. New models pay for results, not time. Before long, most people will be responsible for their own insurance, retirement, and other benefits.

Do not follow where the path may lead.
Go instead where there is no path and leave a trail.
—George Bernard Shaw

What are the QWERTY keyboards in your life? What things are you continuing to do that are no longer effective but have become so habitual you do them anyway?

Stretching Your Thinking

We are often unable to stretch our thinking in new directions because we are limited by our past experience. Just as with our keyboard, we tend to think in predictable ways and see boundaries that may not actually exist. Try these simple mind teasers to help you think in unexpected ways.

1. WHILE BROWSING AROUND on eBay, you see a model car in a glass display case on sale for $200. The car is valued at $190 more than the case. How much is the case worth?

2. THERE ARE SIX MARBLES in a basket. Six children each take one marble. But there is still one marble left in the basket. How can that be?

Revolutionary Insight

The sultan of Persia had sentenced two men to death. One of them, knowing how much the sultan loved his stallion, offered to teach the horse to fly within a year in return for his life. The sultan, fancying himself the rider of the only flying horse in the world, agreed.

The other prisoner looked at his friend in disbelief. "You know horses don't fly. What made you come up with a crazy idea like that? You're only postponing the inevitable." "Not so," said the first prisoner. "I have actually given myself four chances for freedom. First, the sultan might die during the year. Second, I might die. Third, the horse might die. And fourth—I might teach the horse to fly."[4]

Wow! I like this guy's thinking. Rather than giving in to victim mentality and acquiescing to his immediate death, with one creative suggestion he creates four possible outcomes for his future.

3. **You are Driving** in your Porsche on a stormy night when you pass a bus stop and see three people waiting: (1) an old lady who obviously needs help immediately, (2) an old college friend to whom you owe a big favor, and (3) the perfect partner you've been dreaming about. Knowing there's room for only one passenger in your car, whom would you choose for the absolute best results?

4. **Acting on** an anonymous tip, the police close in on a house to arrest a suspected embezzler. They don't know what he looks like; all they know is that his name is Charles. The police rush in and find an attorney, a surgeon, a dentist, and an accountant playing poker. Without hesitation, they arrest the accountant. How can they be so sure?

You will find the answers to these puzzles on page 114.

Even today's job interview questions require a new kind of thinking. Companies like Microsoft, Dell Inc., and Google are asking questions that seem to be unrelated to job performance but help them know how a candidate thinks and solves problems. Here are some examples:

1. What would I find in your refrigerator?
2. Where do you see yourself five years from now?
3. If you were stranded on a desert island and could have only one book, what would it be?

You will find comments on these questions on page 115.

The world hates change, yet it is the only thing that has brought progress.

—Charles F. Kettering

This Is Why Your Job Stinks

Growing up on a farm, I had plenty of time to practice my success principles on our cows. Unfortunately, cows were not very good examples of creative thinking and innovation; rather, they were easy to confuse and control. Scientists have described the standard, unchallenged thinking of humans as "cow paths in the brain." Cows frequently follow one another, usually in a single line, moving along in a very predictable pattern. They do not challenge this pattern, even when it is clearly self-defeating. If an obstacle appears, they will stay where they are, waiting for the obstacle to be removed.

When we were young children, no such paths existed. We took in and processed information in all parts of our brains; we saw seemingly endless options as possibilities. However, as we grew, our brains developed identifiable paths. As we learned to limit the options worth considering, we stopped using our entire brains.

These "cow paths" often keep us from seeing all there is to see. We limit ourselves every day by closing our eyes to the endless variety of opportunities available to us. Statements like "Everybody's laying off" or "Nobody's hiring" or "I don't have enough money to start my own business" or "I'm too old" or "You know you can't get ahead without a college degree" are examples of cow-path thinking.

If you're feeling trapped and think the whole world stinks, it's likely that you are simply stuck on a cow path. Take a small step off that path by thinking creatively about your options and you may see a whole new field of opportunity.

Healers, Dreamers, and Peacemakers

How do we respond to the ever-increasing changes confronting us in the workplace? A *No More Dreaded Mondays* and spiritually creative approach means unlocking the mind and allowing yourself to see a wealth of new and exciting opportunities. God gives us creativity and ingenuity to see solutions that many ignore. There are unlimited opportunities to be leaders, not victims, as the world becomes more complex and our societal problems become increasingly difficult to solve. Our schools need a major overhaul; there is crime in every community; our health care system, families, and churches are full of problems that require new solutions. Many of these issues are suffering from a dearth of originality; they need the creativity and spiritual insight of *No More Dreaded Mondays* thinking. The solutions are not likely to include more information and more technology; rather they can come only from human insight and ingenuity. Even in the career arena,

Revolutionary Insight

Don't Be a Pessimistic Dog

In the 1960s, the psychologist Martin Seligman conducted a series of experiments on optimism and pessimism. In his experiments, dogs would hear a tone and then be given a mild, brief shock. Each dog was then placed in a box with two compartments separated by a low wall. When the tone sounded, the dog would receive a shock that he or she could escape by jumping into the other compartment. Control dogs, which had not been shocked, would easily move from one compartment to the other. However, Seligman found that, upon hearing the tone, the dogs who had previously been shocked would just lie down and whimper. He hypothesized that they had "learned to be helpless." They never learned that they could easily avoid the shock by simply moving to the other side.

The application of Seligman's research: We don't simply respond to the real circumstances around us; rather, our *expectations* largely determine how we respond. Be careful of what you expect. You are likely to end up right there!

one does not have to be a technological genius to survive and prosper. The conventional wisdom, reinforced daily by the business press, is to scramble any way you can to a field with a "future": software, engineering, or global marketing. Otherwise, many warn, you may end up the twenty-first-century equivalent of a blacksmith—trained to do a job that hardly anyone needs.

A lot of what we think of as neurosis in this country is simply people who are unhappy because they are not using their creative resources.

—Julia Cameron

However, the U.S. Bureau of Labor Statistics is struggling to predict accurately the job trends of the next few years. While technological opportunities will continue to exist, the outlook is bleak for people already in those fields who cannot embrace and move with the upcoming changes.

As I wrote in my previous book, *48 Days to the Work You Love*, there has been an explosion of opportunities for *healers, dreamers,* and *peacemakers*. Seventeen of the thirty fastest-growing jobs in the next decade are for healers[5]—and I don't just mean physicians and registered nurses. The number of certified massage therapists has quadrupled since 1990 as the 71.5 million baby boomers suffer increasing minor aches and tensions. The need for counseling therapists will grow dramatically as people entering the second half of their lives confront depression and major life changes. Universally, people are expressing more interest in spiritual matters, giving rise to the need for directors of religious activities and education. Over 100,000 new jobs for clergy and religious directors are expected between 2006 and 2016. The demand for simpler, more humane ways of resolving disputes will expand the opportunities for dispute mediation and arbitration. Ten years ago, there were about 150 dispute mediation centers nationwide;

today, there are at least 500. As baby boomers have approached middle age, enjoying higher education levels and more disposable income, the proportion of boomers who go to a concert, a play, or an art museum at least once a year has risen from 41 percent in 1992 to 63 percent in 2005. The Bureau of Labor Statistics projects that the demand for writers, artists, and entertainers will increase 24 percent over the next decade, with a total of 772,000 new jobs in those fields.[6] If you are gifted in telling a good story, writing a good book, or listening with compassion, there will be opportunities for you.

We are seeing a diminishing of value placed on left-brain skills—analytical, calculating, and detailed. We've learned that computer processes, accounting and financial analysis, database functions, and even medical diagnoses can be done by someone on the other side of the world, while we are sleeping, and for a whole lot less money than is required here. You know what's growing in value in the United States? Right-brain qualities, such as empathy, creativity, artistic skill, adeptness at building relationships, the ability to find joy in oneself and elicit joy in others, the desire to find purpose in life and help others do the same. Today the defining skills of the last ten years—the left-brain skills that launched us into the Information Age—are no longer sufficient. Any job that depends on routine—that can be broken down into a series of repeated steps—is at risk. Jobs that deal in facts and systems may have been readily available, but they are easy to duplicate in China and India. What is beginning to be more valuable is the ability to give those facts human meaning—to add empathy and caring, to provide emotional and spiritual impact. Those right-brain capabilities our culture once thought frivolous will increasingly determine who flourishes and who flounders.

Let me give you an example. One hundred years ago electric lighting was rare; people used candles for evening light. Today lightbulbs are cheap, and we're moving toward using compact fluorescent bulbs that last seven years. Lightbulbs are everywhere, commonplace, no big deal. And candles are long since forgotten, right? Wrong! In the United States alone, candles are a $2.4-billion-a-year industry. There is no *logical* need for candles. So why is their use growing? Because we have a growing desire for beauty and transcendence—qualities that go beyond cold, hard technology. If you can provide beauty and help people have experiences and feelings that go beyond the drudgery of day-to-day existence, you can thrive and become wealthy in the process.

This is not an exhaustive list of new opportunities. But these examples give a quick look at how changes always bring the seeds of new opportunities. As you define your own unique skills, you will also see creative applications that match the emerging trends.

Give me a stock clerk with a dream and I will give you a person who can make history. Give me a person without a dream and I will give you a stock clerk.

—J. C. Penney

Change is inevitable. Our choice is not whether change will occur but, simply, how we will respond. We can choose to wring our hands as victims, convinced opportunities are disappearing, or we can use our awesome creativity to see where new opportunities are appearing and new paths are opening. Each of us has been given unique skills, abilities, personality traits, values, dreams, and passions. As we examine them, we may be surprised at how these "soft" skills can help us become true leaders in industry, entertainment, and humanitarian efforts around the world. We should be at the forefront not only as innovators and inventors but also as peacemakers, healers, and dreamers. If we create individual paths destined by individual purpose and mission, we arm ourselves against corporate downsizing. Rather, we will seize the opportunities and lead the way to higher levels of fulfillment, income, and benefits for those around us.

> *Research shows that 90 percent of five-year-olds are creative, but only 2 percent of adults are.*
>
> —Lee Silber

If you embrace *No More Dreaded Mondays* thinking, you will see solutions that other people may not see and create plans of action that others would find impossible. Old traditions will be exposed as only predictable cow paths rather than as best alternatives.

> *The world will never be happy until all men have the souls of artists—I mean when they take pleasure in their jobs.*
>
> —Auguste Rodin

Answers to the Stretching Your Thinking Mind Teasers

1. If you said the case is worth $10, you are wrong. It's not that simple. If the case is worth $10 and the car is valued at $190 more, then the car would be worth $200 and the total would be $210. The value of the case is actually $5. Therefore, the car is worth $195 and the total is the accurate $200.

2. The sixth child took the basket with the marble still inside.

3. Let the old lady in, of course. Then toss the keys to your friend to get him out of the storm as well. You appear to be the compassionate hero and now get to wait with your perfect partner for the bus, or find another creative solution.

4. The accountant was the only man in the room. The other three were women. (We tend to assume male gender for certain occupations.)

Comments on the Stretching Your Thinking
Interview Questions

1. Obviously, what you have in your refrigerator is not really important. However, this question is an opportunity for the interviewer to see how you handle an unexpected situation. If you are flustered and thrown off track by this question, perhaps anything unexpected in the workplace would cause the same reaction. If you imply that this query has nothing to do with a job application, the interviewer may doubt your openness and willingness to be part of the team.

2. If you respond that five years from now you'd just like to have this same job, the interviewer may question your initiative and desire to improve. But if you say you'd like to have his or her position or be president of the company, the interviewer may assume you would be discontent with the present opportunity. Just clarify your plans for growing and learning—and how you intend to be relevant for new opportunities that may appear at that time.

3. The comedian Steven Wright uses this question in his routine, and he always says the one book he would want is *How to Build a Boat.* You may not be that witty, but you should have a reason for your selection.

If You're a Revolutionary, You Will

- Recognize that "as a man thinketh in his heart, so is he."
- Fire yourself and see nothing but positive possibilities.
- Join the Tigger Factor club.
- Reach for the "opportunity clock" every morning.
- Create settings where you can "hear" God's voice.
- Recognize the cow paths in your routines.

6

"SECURE" OR "IMPRISONED"?

Too many people are thinking of security instead of opportunity.

—James F. Byrnes

The Security of Imprisonment

When Charles Dickens was a small boy, his own father was sent to prison for poverty. As a result, the theme of imprisonment appears repeatedly in his many articles and novels. In one story he wrote about a man who had been in prison for years. Naturally, this man longed for freedom from his dungeon of despair and hopelessness. Finally, the day of his liberation arrived. He was led from his gloomy cell into the bright and beautiful world. He momentarily gazed into the sunlight, then turned and walked back to his cell. He had become so comfortable with confinement that the thought of freedom was overwhelming. For him, the chains and darkness were a predictable security.

How do you view change? Is it frightening and intimidating? Or is it an opportunity for positive transformation?

He who refuses to embrace a unique opportunity loses the prize as surely as if he had failed.

—William James

The first step in creating positive change is to identify what you want. What would your ideal job be? What kind of people would you be working with? What skills would you be using? How would it make a difference in the world? Fortunately, you are not trapped in your job or your life. You can choose to walk into new freedom—or you can choose to stay in your own private prison. Like the man in Dickens's story, we can be tempted to become secure even in negative situations. True freedom is possible only for those who are willing to surrender the security of imprisonment.

This process of defining a clear direction is a very important part of change. Often people come to see me with a very precise sense of what they are *leaving* but no sense of what they are moving *to. As long as you are focused on what you are moving away from, you are likely to experience fear, resentment, anger, or even depression. As soon as you get a clear picture of what you are moving to, you will get a wave of confidence, boldness, and enthusiasm.*

Veering Off Course?

When you were a high school or college student, if you told people you wanted to be an attorney or a physician or a businessperson, you likely had enthusiastic audiences to cheer you on. Parents, teachers, college professors, and friends would encourage, prod, and guide you to success. Similarly, if you are part of a top sales team or a computer programmer or an up-and-coming manager for your firm, you likely attend regular seminars and training programs to build your skills and confidence.

> *There are risks and costs to a program of action. But they are far less than the long-range risks and costs of comfortable inaction.*
>
> —John F. Kennedy

But what if you have decided to move out of the traditional employee role? You've seen the multitude of new opportunities that aren't about just clocking in, having an hour for lunch, a two-week vacation, and a predictable paycheck. You're imagining taking greater control of your time and income. Now who cheers you on? Who guides you? Who tells you how to be successful, and when to show up for work? Do your coworkers, bosses, family, and friends encourage you, or do they think you are crazy to entertain the idea of something new? Do they admire your determination or tell you that what you want to do is not *practical* or *realistic*? When problems arise, they may not be that sympathetic. After all, you chose to be a risk taker, to leave the security, predictability, and stability of a "real job."

You may hesitate to discuss your concerns with those you know best. They have their own problems and pressures. Sometimes it's even hard to share your excitement because your success may just remind others of the misery of their own work.

> *The quality of the imagination is to flow and not to freeze.*
>
> —Ralph Waldo Emerson

With the current explosion in revolutionary workplace environments, one term we're seeing a lot is *free agent*. That's pretty easy to understand, and it's an accurate representation of someone who has the luxury of looking at many options. In *Free Agent Nation,* Daniel Pink wrote, "If the term is vague, it is because I can think of no other way to describe the people I am talking about. They are free from the bonds of a large institution, and agents of their own futures. They are the new archetypes of work in America. Today, in the shadow of another economic boom, America's new economic emblem is the footloose, independent worker— the tech-savvy, self-reliant, path-charting micropreneur."[1] The trends Pink predicted in 2001 have proven to be accurate and dramatic. We are seeing traditional university programs threatened as people take advantage of new and quicker methods of gaining needed work skills. As free agents, more Americans are electing to bypass retirement, choosing instead to continue work they find exciting and fulfilling. The growth of new opportunities has not been for the tech-savvy only; there has also been a resurgence of simple service businesses that provide needed conveniences for the baby boomer generation. Cottage industries have exploded; 20 million Americans are now considered "solo entrepreneurs."

As you move into work of your choosing and design, work that integrates your strongest talents and unique gifts, you will experience a joy not commonly connected with "work." You'll find that your desire to quit and move into the blank slate of retirement will diminish significantly.

More and more Americans are looking for greater control over their destinies and for the time freedom that working independently allows. But freedom alone isn't enough. Your work must integrate your skills, your personality, and your interests. That may seem obvious, but it is amazing how often these simple principles are violated. The more you understand about yourself and match that knowledge up with your work goals and direction, the more you increase your chances for success.

Are You Sabotaging Yourself?

If you think and make decisions like yesterday's employee, being in the driver's seat becomes an agonizing experience. Customers don't buy when they've indicated they will, equipment breaks

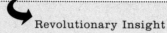

Revolutionary Insight

Here's an e-mail I received.

> *Dan, I am a fan who has been reading your emails for a long time. We desperately need your advice. . . . My husband has been offered a buyout from General Motors to leave a job that he really hates! We just returned from Georgia where we looked into buying a business. We found a suitable place and I am very excited but he is reluctant to leave a decent paying job with decent benefits to grow a business where we would go to paying for all insurances etc. Any advice?? By the way, he has to make his decision in the next two weeks! If he leaves, he would receive $140,000, before taxes, four weeks later.*
>
> *Thanks for any help,* Fans in Michigan

Wow—how often does the opportunity to be paid $140,000 to leave a job you hate appear? Working in a job you hate never makes sense in the long term—even if you have to pay to leave. That being said, this seems to be a pretty easy decision. General Motors is eliminating positions left and right—certainly no job security there anymore. And to already have a business idea means you aren't just leaving—you're moving toward a new chapter in your lives. Most people who go through this kind of change look back two years later and wonder why they didn't do it much sooner.

when you least expect it, workers don't show up as planned, and the landlord raises the rent unexpectedly. In many ways, the characteristics that make a good employee are often the exact opposites of those that make a successful Revolutionary. Being loyal and predictable and doing what others expect may, in fact, sabotage your best efforts.

While there is no question that college prepares would-be doctors and lawyers, a college degree is not necessarily a good

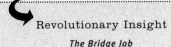

Revolutionary Insight

The Bridge Job

• Baby boomers are turning sixty at the rate of one every ten seconds. But as life spans lengthen, pensions crumble, and retirement boredom beckons, more American workers find it less desirable to drop from full-time work to full-time leisure in one quick move. Enter the "bridge job." This is a term being used to describe part-time or even full-time jobs held for fewer than ten years following lengthy careers.

• According to a 2005 working paper from the Center on Aging & Work at Boston College, one-half to two-thirds of workers take on bridge jobs before fully retiring. And this is one reason the number of workers age sixty-five and up is expected to increase 117 percent by 2025. "Why go from one hundred miles per hour to zero?" asks Joseph Quinn, a Boston College economist and coauthor of the paper. "You wouldn't do that in your car. You'd do seventy, then fifty, then twenty."

• Bridge jobs can be advantageous for both the worker and the company. The worker continues to be productive and generate some income. The company gets the full value of work experience and knows the worker isn't looking for long-term employment or benefits.

predictor for Revolutionary success. Research shows that the true predictors of success have little to do with education. Incidentally, the following list of the real predictors of success references some notable college dropouts.

If one advances confidently in the direction of his dreams, and endeavors to live the life which he has imagined, he will meet with a success unexpected in common hours.

—Henry David Thoreau

The Five Predictors of Success

1. Passion

Bill Gates was able to build Microsoft and become the richest man in the world because he was passionate about his vision of putting "a computer on every desk in every home." Passion, defined as intense emotional excitement, goes beyond mere enthusiasm.

HOW PASSION PREDICTS SUCCESS A person with passion is a person who can set goals. Without them, you'll have no clear direction and will drift along the road of circumstances. Another technology visionary, Steve Jobs, cofounder of Apple Computer, abandoned his studies at Reed College to pursue more lucrative goals. Once he identified his passion, he was impatient with a slow path to carrying it out. You, too, can recognize your passions. When you share your goals with others, however, don't be surprised to hear responses like "Yes, but that's not realistic" or "That's not practical."

> *You see things and say "Why?" But I dream things that never were and say "Why not?"*
>
> —George Bernard Shaw

Larry Dobbs dropped out of school at age fifteen. His passion was to work on cars. While tinkering with the cars he loved, he also started a newsletter for fellow Mustang lovers called *Mustang Monthly*. That little newsletter grew into an automotive publishing company with eight titles. In 1999, after being wooed by multiple buyers, he sold the company that was an extension of his passion. Dobbs Publishing Group was purchased by Petersen Companies for $18 million.

2. Determination

In her autobiography, titled *Dolly*, Dolly Parton says, "My high school was small. So during a graduation event, each of us got a chance to stand up and announce our plans for the future. 'I'm going to junior college,' one boy would say. 'I'm getting married and moving to Maryville,' a girl would follow. When my turn came, I said, 'I'm going to Nashville to become a star.' The entire place erupted in laughter. I was stunned. Somehow, though, that laughter instilled in me an even greater determination to realize my dream. I might have crumbled under the weight of the hardships that were to come had it not been for the response of the crowd that day. Sometimes it's funny the way we find inspiration."[2]

That little girl went on to write over three thousand songs. Today, Dolly, the fourth of twelve children, holds the record for the number of awards for a female country artist—including seven Grammys and an Emmy. In 1986, the year her theme park, Dollywood, opened, gross business revenues for the city of Pigeon Forge, Tennessee, jumped 47 percent. Her Imagination Library program has been adopted in six hundred communities in forty-one states. With her triple skills as a businesswoman, entertainer, and philanthropist, Dolly is respectfully referred to as the "Tennessee Icon."

HOW DETERMINATION PREDICTS SUCCESS Without determination, a person can easily be lured away from his or her path. Many years ago, Viktor Frankl said, "Without a clear purpose, any obstacle will send a person in a new direction." Stephen Covey, in *The 7 Habits of Highly Effective People*, talks about the tendency to respond to circumstances rather than priorities. Just recognize that, if you respond to circumstances, any obstacle will send you off in a new direction. But with determination, you can establish priorities that will guide you through even challenging and unexpected circumstances.

Richard Branson, founder of the Virgin Group, whose endeavors include record publishing, airlines, and a host of other businesses, was a high school dropout and a millionaire by the age of twenty-three. How? By not seeing his lack of formal schooling as an obstacle to accomplishing his goals. His first business venture was at age sixteen, when he published a magazine called *Student*. Today, his net worth is estimated at over $8 billion, according to the Sunday *Times* Rich List.[3] Incidentally, in 1993, Branson received an honorary doctor of technology from Loughborough University. In 1999, he became Sir Richard Branson when he was knighted by the Queen of England for "services to entrepreneurship."

You may identify determination even in a child if, for example, she is able to delay gratification by saving her allowance for a future goal instead of spending it now. In the 1960s, Walter Mischel conducted a now-famous experiment at Stanford University. Four-year-olds were given a marshmallow and promised another, if only they could wait twenty minutes before eating the first one. Some children could wait and others could not. The researchers then followed all the children into adolescence and demonstrated that those with the ability to wait were better adjusted and more dependable, and scored an average of 210 points higher on the Scholastic Aptitude Test.[4]

So are you swayed by today's circumstances or determined to pursue worthy long-term goals?

All men of action are dreamers.
—James G. Huneker

---

3. Talent

As a young boy, Walt Disney lived in the world of fantasy and entertainment. When he first approached a Kansas City newspaper with his drawings, the editor told him, "These won't do. If I were you, I'd give up this work. From these sketches, it's obvious your talent lies elsewhere." Walt could have easily given up. Here was a known "expert" telling him he had no talent for cartooning. He could have made excuses for not pursuing his dream to draw and write. All he could find for a studio was an old mouse-infested garage, but in that garage Walt continued to draw his cartoons. We all know how one of those mice became an international household word. Talent is a funny thing. If you wait for perfect conditions, it will likely never appear.

HOW TALENT PREDICTS SUCCESS Talent allows a person to focus. No one has talent in every area; discover where you rise to the top. What are those things you love to do whether or not you get paid?

Sometimes we discover that our first sense of calling is guided more by others' expectations than by our strongest areas of competence. Ron felt called to be a pastor. Yet his call proved to be a continually frustrating experience. After taking a fresh look at God's real gifts to him, he began to create faux finishes on the walls of expensive homes in his area. Using brushes, sponges, and rags, he creates beautiful and dramatic effects, expressing his talent and helping bring people's dream homes to life. He keeps a six- to nine-month backlog of commissioned work and is making approximately ten times the money he was in his former work. And he told me recently that his opportunities for ministry have been dramatically expanded as he is authentically utilizing God's unique gifts to him.

There's always free cheese in a mousetrap.

—Old proverb

---

4. Self-Discipline

Years ago, Jenny Craig was faced with losing forty-five pounds.

While taking off the weight, she gained the self-discipline she needed to launch her own company. Her estimated annual company sales today? $400 million.

HOW SELF-DISCIPLINE PREDICTS SUCCESS Without self-discipline, a person can easily be swayed by others. Self-discipline is the foundation that makes the other predictors work. Knowing the other predictors is the initial step, but acting on them always requires self-discipline. However, don't assume this acting means hardship and suffering—rather, it will be a joy to be focused and intentional while others around you evidence their floundering lives with wasted time and resources.

As an author, poet, and actress, Maya Angelou has been a powerful voice in the American civil rights movement. She was named one of the thirty most powerful women in America by *Ladies' Home Journal* in 2001. But she never would have accomplished all she has done without persistence. A childhood trauma led her to restrict her speaking and writing until age thirteen. Although discouraged by others even years later, she persisted with her autobiographical writing, what eventually became her acclaimed book *I Know Why the Caged Bird Sings*. Today, she enjoys over $4 million in yearly income.

> *If a man empties his purse into his head, no man can take it away from him. An investment in knowledge always pays the best interest.*
>
> —Benjamin Franklin

5. Faith

Even with everything lining up logically or financially, real success requires that step of faith into the unknown. You've no doubt heard of Thomas Edison's ten thousand failed attempts to invent the lightbulb. Even passion, determination, talent, and self-discipline would not have carried him on. He had to believe that if God had allowed him to see it in his mind, it could become a physical reality. I might add that Edison had this to say about the faith that kept him going: "Faith, as well intentioned as it may be, must be built on facts, not fiction—faith in fiction is a damnable false hope."

Time and time again we see examples of people who, in the face of all odds, continued because of their confident assurance of what was coming.

HOW FAITH PREDICTS SUCCESS Faith is that intangible ingredient that moves a person past the initial planning and persistence. Success is ultimately more art than science, more intuition than logic. "What is faith? It is the confident assurance that something we want is going to happen. It is the certainty that what we hope for is waiting for us, even though we cannot see it up ahead. Men of God in days of old were famous for their faith" (Hebrews 11:1-2, TLB).

As a young boy, Norman Vincent Peale fought against strong feelings of inferiority. Over the years he developed and refined the message that all people could put the principles of positive thinking and strong faith into practice and dramatically improve their lives. His book *The Power of Positive Thinking* has sold nearly 20 million copies and been printed in forty different languages.

Albert Einstein did not speak until he was four years old and did not read until he was seven. His parents thought he was "subnormal," and one of his teachers described him as "mentally slow, unsociable, and adrift forever in foolish dreams." He was considered a slow learner, possibly because of dyslexia, autism, or the unusual structure of his brain (examined after his death).[5] He later credited his development of the theory of relativity to this slowness, saying that by pondering space and time later than most children, he was able to apply to them a more developed intellect. He was awarded the 1921 Nobel Prize in Physics for his explanation of the photoelectric effect.

As you can see, the criteria for success as a Revolutionary are much more internal than external. It is easy to identify areas of opportunity in today's world; however, those will have little bearing on your success until you know yourself.

The more you know about yourself, the higher your chances of success as a Revolutionary. Your security does not come from a company, the government, or your hoped-for retirement or pension plan. You must shift from looking at external factors to looking at internal ones. This is also a shift from waiting for a break to making your own breaks.

As George Bernard Shaw observed, while people blame circumstances for the condition of their lives, "the people who get on in this world are the people who get up and look for the circumstances they want, and, if they can't find them, make them." Nowhere is this truer than when you're working for yourself.

> Our hearts have to join our heads to find true life direction. Destiny is not a matter of chance; it is a matter of choice. It is not a thing to be waited for; it is a thing to be achieved.
>
> —William Jennings Bryan

There are two major principles to choose from when looking for a revolutionary idea.

1. FIND A NEED AND FILL IT. Anything that provides speed, convenience, or efficiency for the baby boomer generation can make you rich. Many years ago, a typist was frustrated by the inconvenience of making so many corrections. Often the paper tore as errors were being erased, making it necessary to start over. To remedy the situation, this woman began mixing white flour with clear fingernail polish. She would use this mixture to cover her typing mistakes, finding that it would dry quickly and allow her

to type over the same area again. Other workers began asking her for this concoction she was preparing each night on her kitchen table. Four years later, she sold her little "business" to Gillette for $47 million, leading to what became Liquid Paper.

2. FIND A PROBLEM AND SOLVE IT. How can you provide a solution? How can you offer something quicker, cheaper, better? At our office, a young man started coming around every Tuesday and Friday to pick up and deliver our dry cleaning. What he picked up on Tuesday, he brought back on Friday, and Friday's

> ## ↶ Revolutionary Insight
>
> In his book *Rich Dad, Poor Dad*, Robert Kiyosaki tells the story of the Hawaiian black crabs. If you go down to the beach early in the morning, you can find black crabs. You can put them in your bucket and continue walking on the beach. Now those crabs start thinking, We are bumping around in this little bucket making a lot of noise but going nowhere. Eventually, one crab looks up and thinks, There's a whole new world up there. If I could just get my foot up over the edge, I could get out, get my freedom, and see the world in my own way. So he stretches up, pushes a little, and sure enough, gets one foot over the edge. But just as he is about to tip the balance, a crab from the bottom of the bucket reaches up and pulls him back. Instead of encouraging him and seeing how they could help one another get to freedom, the crabs pull anyone attempting to get out back down into that confining bucket, where death will come quickly.
>
> Unfortunately, many of us live around a bunch of black crabs, ready to ridicule any new idea we have and just as eager to pull us back down to their level of performance. I have found that one of the key characteristics of successful people is that they hang around people who are performing at the level at which they want to perform. There will always be naysayers and whiners; avoid them. Find winners and spend time with them![6]

pickup would be returned on the next Tuesday. We were probably passing five to six dry cleaners on the way to work each day, but the convenience of his service made us loyal customers. He does not do the dry cleaning, only the pickup and delivery. We pay normal rates for the dry cleaning; for bringing the dry cleaners new business, he receives 40 percent of the revenue. Given that the cleaner makes approximately $20,000 monthly in gross business from all his new customers, this young man takes home $8,000 a month for his services. He is now offering that simple idea, with a clear plan, as a business opportunity to others. He has identified a need, recognized his talent for relationship selling, and turned those into a very profitable part of his calling.

> *Most great businesses were built with sweat equity.*
> *Do something small and build it slowly.*

Look for the multiple options in any situation. Don't assume too quickly that there are only two or even three possibilities. If you despise your boss, you could

1. Quit your job.
2. Ask for a transfer.
3. Learn to love your boss.
4. Buy the company and fire the boss.
5. Throw your back out playing golf and go on disability.
6. Join the Marines.
7. Go back to school.
8. Marry the boss's daughter or her son.
9. Praise the boss's work to facilitate a promotion for him or her.
10. Volunteer for a demotion.

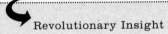

Revolutionary Insight

And This Donkey Died Because . . .

You may know the medieval logic dilemma of the donkey that is placed equidistant from two piles of food of equal size and quality—a perfectly symmetrical situation. If the behavior of the donkey were completely rational, the donkey would have no reason to prefer one pile to the other; therefore, it could not decide which pile to eat first. So it would remain in its original position and starve to death. This dilemma is called "Buridan's ass."

I find many people immobilized by the challenge of choosing—even if both choices are attractive. Two great schools, two great jobs, two great business ideas. In my graduate psychology brainstorming groups, we would create what-if scenarios. What if the donkey, aware that he is starving, flips a coin to make a choice? Which pile of food is heads and which is tails? Ah yes, another decision.

If you are looking at two opportunities, how do you ultimately make the decision? If you are considering moving to Denver or Miami, how do you make that call? If you have been accepted by Harvard and the Peace Corps, what will help you choose?

The trick is that there aren't two choices here, there are three: If you choose not to decide, you still have made a choice. It's just as obvious a choice as either of the new options. So you may as well make it interesting by changing the scenery.

Remember this sequence for making a choice: (1) Clearly state the issue. (2) Get the advice and opinions of others. (3) List your options. (4) Choose the best option. Even if the options seem equally attractive, you must choose one. (5) *Act*. Don't be a donkey; you just might starve as a result of your indecision. And indecision in one area will cripple your effectiveness in all other areas.

A double-minded man is unstable in all his ways.

—James 1:8

Some options are clearly more attractive than others, and I'm confident you could think of several more as well. The point is, you always have multiple choices. There is never one option only. More often than not, you have more choices than you first think.

Practice; be prepared; see everything you do as training; invest time working for a similar company; get experience. See what you have already done as valuable preparation for your next venture.

> *The way to succeed is to double your failure rate.*
> —Thomas Watson, founder of IBM

Here is the process you should follow in developing a *No More Dreaded Mondays* attitude:

1. Set a specific *goal*.
2. Start *small* and build your idea slowly.
3. Test every move.
4. Expand on the basis of your success.
5. Carefully select the right people to help you grow.

The most important thing is to begin. Fear of failure can immobilize you, even with a great idea. Only about one in ten people who want to work more independently ever do. Fear of failure paralyzes people and makes failure certain.

> *Do what you fear and fear disappears.*
> —W. Clement Stone

If You're a Revolutionary, You Will
- Recognize prisons of your own making.
- Clarify what you are moving *to*.
- Be able to describe yourself as a "free agent."
- See in yourself the Five Predictors of Success.
- Allow your faith to expand and fuel your dreams.
- Identify opportunities to fill a need or solve a problem.
- Not get caught in indecision; you will make a choice and move on.

7

BUT YOU OWE ME

Bigger = Better?

On the farm where I grew up, we struggled to survive financially. We started with one cow and slowly built up a milking herd, with the milking initially done by hand. Eventually, we got milking machines and better tractors for the field work, but the days were still long and exhausting. As a thirteen-year-old, I stressed my back loading hay bales, and I have spent every day since then trying to compensate for that injury. And the financial payoff for this hard work was minimal. Only after Dad's yearly income grew to about seven thousand dollars was he able to pay off that thirteen-thousand-dollar farm purchase.

I saw college as my escape from the hard work and financial limitations of farm life. Upon graduating from Ohio State University, I got a "real job" at a private psychiatric hospital. Not only was I a college graduate, and with a job where I didn't have to strain my back and stay dirty all day, but they were willing to pay me $6,700 a year, an amount that it took my dad decades of backbreaking work to attain. The work was rewarding and stimulating. As a member of the adjunctive therapy team, I was seen as a professional, and my work was valued by many. Yet I quickly began to see some limitations there. If I just showed up on time and went through the motions, I got my paycheck. If I showed up early and stayed late, studied on my own, and offered new methods for more effective treatment, I got exactly the same pay-check. I talked to people who had been on the staff for many years and were still making pretty much what I was as a new-comer.

I saw that, if I wanted more open-ended possibilities, I was going to have to explore different ways of working. But I also saw that, if I took responsibility for the results, I could open the door for financial rewards. I returned to graduate school, got my mas-ter's in psychology, and paved the way for my exodus from the traditional job forever. Over time I purchased, started, and ran "normal" businesses, including auto accessories sales, fitness cen-ters, and used car sales. Along the way, I studied the growing number of options for creating income.

Seventeen years ago I had forty-six employees in two busi-nesses. Today I have seven income streams and no full-time em-ployees. Yes, I do use the services of approximately thirty competent people who are paid for their direct contributions to my businesses, but they are not employees. And yes, trust me, my bottom-line profits today are substantially greater than they were back then. People question me frequently about how it is possible to grow a business without having bigger buildings and more and more employees. The key is to develop systems—then find the brightest and best to operate those systems.

Warren Buffett is America's second richest individual. He runs his $136 billion company, Berkshire Hathaway Inc., from a small office in Omaha with the notable absence of a computer. He shuns meetings and spent most of a recent Wednesday working on new lyrics to "Love Me Tender" for a birthday party for his friend Bill Gates. Despite having substantial stakes in Coca-Cola, Wells Fargo, American Express, and countless other companies, Berkshire has no public relations, human resources, or legal de-partments. Its headquarters is staffed by just seventeen employ-ees. Mr. Buffett occasionally carries a cell phone but does not use one when he's in his home city. He keeps no calculator on his

POT-SHOTS
Brilliant Thoughts in 17 Words or Less

desk, preferring to do most calculations in his head. He also has allowed about $40 billion in cash to accumulate at Berkshire because he hasn't found many attractive companies to invest in during the last couple of years.

His methods defy most popular business models. But Mr. Buffett has obviously figured out some ways to have a successful business without the normally expected elements. In this chapter I will clarify the important distinctions between time-and-effort and results-based compensation. You will be reminded that the common model of being paid for time is very recent historically. Real-world economics do not support that model— and there are attractive alternatives once a person understands them.

Time and Effort versus Results

We tend to equate time with productivity; however, in today's work environment, there may be little connection between the two. The factory worker who, with overtime, averages ten hours a day may make $50,000 a year. What about the twenty-four-

year-old with a sports information Internet site? He may spend
two hours a day updating information available to most of the
world. At a site subscription fee of $4.95 per month, he may have
10,000 subscribers. That's almost $50,000 *a month*. How is this
disparity possible? It's because we are seeing a transition from a
time-and-effort economy to a *results-based economy*. You may have
three unique pet products for which you hold distribution rights.
Or maybe you have an eBay connection for antique gold equipment. Strategically placed magazine ads can fuel purchases that
generate a $10,000-a-month income while you spend the major-
ity of your time on the golf course or at the beach.

In order to survive in the coming revolution, we must think
creatively, find new solutions, develop new products, and change
much of what we were doing last year. And we must be careful
of thinking we've made the leap to the new world when we
haven't. Today many people are sitting in Dilbert cubicles with
every keystroke on their computers timed and perfected, thinking they are on the cutting edge of information and technology,
and thus security. But rather than being in a solid position for the
future, they may just be in a vulnerable factory job where they
don't get dirty.

Let's step back in time a bit. If you had approached a wagon
maker a hundred years ago and asked him to build you a wagon,
how would you have arranged payment? Would you have guaranteed him thirty thousand dollars a year with benefits and perhaps helped with his retirement plan? Or at least assured him of
a reasonable hourly rate while he worked on the construction of
your wagon? Of course not! You would only have agreed on a
price for the finished product—a hundred dollars, or thirty clams,
whatever.

When America was young, these cottage industries were the
rule rather than the exception. If you were a baker, you probably sold baked goods to your neighbors. Blacksmiths, candlestick
makers, doctors, and farmers practiced their trades close to or at

home. Their customers were nearby, and they were paid for their results, not their time.

> *All I've ever wanted was an honest week's pay for an honest day's work.*
>
> —Steve Martin

It was only with the beginning of assembly-line factories that we saw guaranteed hourly or annual wages. Work environments were created where people had little direct responsibility for the finished product, and thus they were compensated for their time and effort. In 1907, Henry Ford announced his goal for the Ford Motor Company to create "a motor car for the great multitude." He developed the assembly-line system, in which all parts were interchangeable—any steering wheel would fit any chassis, any valve would fit in any engine, et cetera. With this repetitive system, he was able to hire low-skilled laborers to replace the skilled craftsmen who formerly made the parts by hand. Mr. Ford was considered a Revolutionary when he suggested paying his workers a guaranteed $2.50 a day. Thus began the "paycheck mentality" that is prevalent in today's work environment (I put in my time; thus you owe me). And many organizations are simply saying they will no longer tolerate such a guarantee.

In 1914, Ford workers' wages were raised to five dollars a day, nearly double what was offered by other industrial plants. Henry Ford was called "a traitor to his class" by other industrialists, but he held firm in *believing that well-paid workers would put up with dull work, be loyal, and buy his cars.*[1] And there you have the basis for paying for time rather than results. If you are guaranteed income for the time you put in, it's theoretically because you are doing dull, repetitive work that could be done by many low-skilled laborers. What we are seeing today is simply a healthy return to a results-based economy. And with that return comes an opportunity to be compensated for results—which may not have a direct correlation to time invested.

When you become a Revolutionary and break out of the traditional employee model, the rules do change. You may suggest to your current boss that your compensation switch to a salary based on results rather than time. You may suggest that you could just as easily work from home, thus saving the company rent, utilities, and liability for your work space. You may decide to focus on the area of your current job in which you're most skilled—graphic design or high-level accounting—still receive a salary from your current employer for that specialty, and open the door to two or three additional clients. These options do not necessitate burning bridges; you may be able to create a very subtle change in your work model and continue doing your current work.

There may be no one to tell you when to get up, when to eat, when to take breaks, how long to work, or whether to work at all. But keep clearly in mind—results get compensated. Results translate into money. When you get started, there won't be a guaranteed paycheck, but results generate money and, frequently, lots of it. Revolutionaries will enjoy the benefits of new opportunities and higher levels of compensation as well as the joys of realized purpose and meaningful work.

He that will not apply new remedies must expect new evils.
—Francis Bacon

Begin to see in the changes around you opportunities rather than the elimination of potential security and predictable income. This is a recurring theme in *No More Dreaded Mondays*—that opportunity lies in seeing things with new eyes.

> *It is only with the heart that one can see rightly. What is essential is invisible to the eye.*
>
> —Antoine de Saint-Exupéry

Lost Job = New Opportunity

Let's create our own scenario from a few millennia ago: ten cavemen spend their days fishing. Each morning the ten men go down to the local lake, cast their lines, and hope to provide the necessary food for their dependents. Then one day, Barney shows up with a net he has fashioned from strings and ropes. Because the net can capture even the fish who escape the lure of the fishing lines, Barney is able to catch more fish in one hour than he and his ten friends had been catching all day. Suddenly Barney can supply fish for the whole village. So what happens to the other ten fishermen? Are they out of work? Do they now have nothing of value to occupy their time? Do they give up working and start receiving three clams a day as unemployment compensation? Should their village guarantee their children's education and their families' medical care as they sit idly by in their front yards? Or are there other new opportunities that may even complement the services of Barney and his new fishing net?

Let's create some possibilities for those ten fishermen.

1. Clem. Clem is no dummy. He's Barney's younger brother, and he sees an opportunity. He starts making more nets like the one Barney is using. As word spreads, he hires ten people to help make the nets.

2. Oscar. Because of the quantity of fish now being caught, Oscar opens a fish-processing plant at the edge of the lake. He brings on fifteen people to help, as they begin to ship to inland areas whose residents have never before eaten fresh fish.

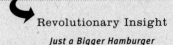

Revolutionary Insight

Just a Bigger Hamburger

What's the difference between a $6-an-hour McDonald's clerk and a $300-an-hour attorney? Not as much as you might think. In both cases, as soon as they walk out the door, their income stops. The attorney may have more toys and a bigger house, but unless he or she is a partner, neither has any leverage in his or her earning ability. Both are trapped in linear income. I recently worked with a dentist who makes in excess of $35,000 monthly—but he works so much that he has no life beyond his job. Furthermore, if he's not at the office, his income stops. How smart is that?

Lots of ideas create residual income. That's the appeal of multilevel-marketing companies; it's what celebrities get from endorsements, what authors get in royalties, and what you can get from being a distributor for jelly beans, selling comic books online, having a yard-mowing business with three employees, starting a co-op buying service for dentists, or hosting an Internet site with information on pet insurance. There are thousands of ways to make at least a thousand dollars a month without stepping foot in an office.

3. **Henry.** Given the need for transportation, Henry begins to build wagons to haul the fish to other parts of the country. He can't keep up with the demand by himself, so he hires five people to help him build wagons (perhaps the precursors to the SUV).

4. **Bill.** Bill sees the opportunity to be the driver of the wagons hauling the fish. But he can drive only one personally, so he hires six other people for separate delivery routes.

5. **Charlie.** Since so many moms and dads are now working in these new enterprises, the children are not being taught their lessons. Charlie and his wife, Sarah, recognize the need and open

the Friendship School of Cave City. To help them in the teaching process, they hire and train six assistants.

6. RONALD. More and more people are working away from home and do not have time to fix their own meals. So Ronald opens Bedrock's first restaurant. Guess what his specialty is? Right, fresh fish. Ronald hires fifteen people with rotating shifts to help out with the cooking, serving, and cleaning.

7. LEVI. As workers are moving in new circles, seeing more strangers each day, they recognize that the fig leaf is not appropriate attire for every occasion, especially for working in proximity to the saws in the wagon factory. Levi begins designing a new clothing option for those workers, something durable and protective—thus Levi's jeans are born. Levi brings on twelve people immediately because the demand for his products is so great.

8. CYRUS. As the number of net builders, wagon carpenters, and drivers increases, people have less time to grow their own basic food. Cyrus forms a co-op with eight others to begin a commercial farming operation. They grow wheat, carrots, peas, and beans. They also have a small orchard to supplement the vegetables and grains with an occasional piece of fruit.

9. ROMAN. This man, who began working on the farm, discovers one day, quite by accident, that the wheat can be ground up and used in other ways. By cooking the ground wheat, Roman invents what he calls "bread." Word spreads quickly that bread goes well with cheese and fish, and Roman has to hire eighteen people to help him handle the orders.

10. MULAH. So many clams are changing hands every day that the average person has trouble keeping track of what clams are his and what are part of the business. Mulah, after training himself, hires five others, teaches them the principles of handling clams, and opens the first bank.

> *There is nothing permanent except change.*
> —Heraclitus

This has always been the process of innovation. Throughout history, society's problem solvers have been generously rewarded for their efforts. Instead of the fishing net putting 10 people out of work, the innovations in this small village led to the employment of 110 people in meaningful work. Today's work environment is very similar. As always before in our history, we need creative people to see the opportunities instead of obstacles, and to create the future. And today, as in every stage of our country's development, the best opportunities may not look like those of yesterday. Today's best opportunities may not include punching a clock, having a company car, or being guaranteed health insurance and a retirement plan. They may not involve an eight-to-five schedule or even an office.

What opportunities can you see in your current work environment? Do you see the need for more convenience for your coworkers? Would they be thrilled to have some healthy snack options at 10:30 and 2:30 each day? Would they be candidates for chair massages? Do you see a machine that needs an improved design? What about doing oil changes and car cleanups for all those cars sitting in the parking lot all day? Do you have an eye for fashion? Could you help your coworkers shop to look their very best? Could you teach business etiquette, showing the importance of eye contact, smile, and tone of voice? People have made fortunes with all of these and many other simple ideas, like Post-it notes, the stapler, Starbucks coffee, the PalmPilot—the list goes on and on. What are ten ideas you've had but have not acted upon?

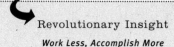

Revolutionary Insight

Work Less, Accomplish More

Great musicians claim that their music comes to life because of the spaces between the notes. Artists use the dark areas to bring the colors to life. Similarly, the spaces between moments you spend working allow ideas and solutions to incubate and grow.

When Leonardo da Vinci was working on *The Last Supper,* he spent many days on the scaffold, painting from dawn till dusk; then, without warning, he would take a break for a few days. The prior of Santa Maria delle Grazie, who'd contracted for his services, was not amused. He would beg Leonardo to continue with the work. He preferred that Leonardo be "just like the labourers hoeing in the garden, never to have laid down his brush." Leonardo tried to persuade the old gentleman that "the greatest geniuses sometimes accomplish more when they work less."[2]

Why Profits Are Better Than Wages

This is a tough issue. Our culture teaches us to expect wages for our time—the person who makes ten dollars an hour wants twelve, the attorney who makes a hundred dollars an hour wants to work his or her way up to two hundred, and so on. Whatever the level, we're talking about wages, or linear income. Is your income linear or residual? Here's how you can tell. Just ask yourself this question: How many times do I get paid for every hour I work? If you answered, "Only once," then your income is *linear*—you are making wages. Salaries offer linear income. Doctors and dentists earn linear income. Linear income is very time dependent—typically, when you don't show up for work, or you take a day off, your paycheck stops.

With *residual* income (profits), you work hard once and it unleashes a steady flow of income for months or even years. You get paid over and over again for the same effort.

I continue to see people who have been let go by major companies become angry that, after twenty or twenty-five years of working for security, they are now left out in the cold. No matter how wonderful your company is, if you're making a linear income, you are not secure; you only have the illusion of security. Working as an employee, with no connection to the profits you help bring in, is not security. It's just *the illusion of security.* Working for a company is fine, but you must understand that doing so will never give you security.

You can work for linear income and still create residual income in other ways. Investment, real estate, inventions, writing, small business, Internet marketing, visual arts, software development, and network marketing are just a few areas that offer potential residual income. With these examples you can see the potential of working for a company while also creating your own residual income.

Something changes when you start working for profits rather than wages. I've seen the guy who'd always been too tired to go to work become motivated to stay up all night placing his baseball cards for sale on eBay. Or the woman who'd felt depressed and exhausted all week spend forty energetic hours on the weekend writing her first novel.

I've seen a person's attitude, voice, and face change when he or she starts to embrace this new way of working. The possibility of profits is empowering and releases the deepest reserves of creativity and energy. Working for wages is limiting—the temptation is to do the very least to maintain the predictable and limited reward.

Three Income-Generating Options

Here are three clear options for generating income (each one has a correlation between time and income). The line in each graph shows the expected income path.

Option 1

Traditional job. Guaranteed income and benefits. Linear income. Clear exchange of time and effort. (Keep in mind that with any guarantee there is a trade-off of opportunities.)

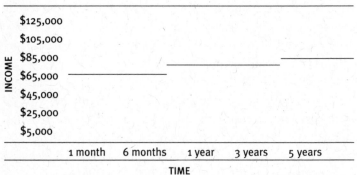

This is a picture of the traditional job. You are guaranteed a paycheck from Week 1. You go to work at 8:00 in the morning and get off at 5:00 in the afternoon. You have an hour off for lunch, receive a paycheck every other Friday, and have two weeks of vacation each year. You have medical insurance, a 401(k) contribution plan, and other benefits provided. You receive a periodic pay increase, perhaps a company incentive, or you get promoted to the next level. Big moves up or down in income are unlikely.

Example: Sarah got her certification as a medical technician in 2004. She started a job at $32,000 per year and was delighted. Today she still enjoys her work, but her pay has not even kept pace with inflation. Having received 3 to 4 percent periodic increases, common for her profession, she now makes $34,000 per year and is having trouble paying daily living expenses for herself and her two children.

Option 2

Base salary with bonuses and commissions based on performance. This could be a sales position or other such positions where at least part of the compensation is tied to performance. This is an increasingly common model, even for traditional employee positions.

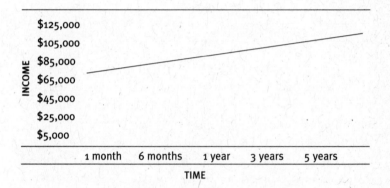

In this option you receive a base salary, perhaps less than what you are used to making but, nonetheless, a salary. However, you have the potential to increase your income greatly, either through your direct efforts or through the success of the company. You are thus helping to share the *risk*.

Example: Chuck went to work for Burlington Carpet, calling on commercial accounts. He was given $56,000 a year base pay with incentives for his sales efforts. Now, five years later, Chuck is making $110,000 a year as a result of successful relationships with his customers and his ability to recognize and fulfill their needs.

Option 3

No guarantees, no paychecks, but the potential is unlimited; it is, in fact, results-oriented.

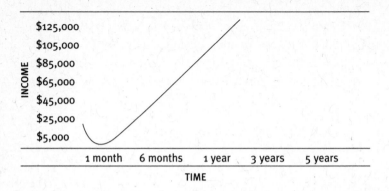

With this option, you are on your own. As you can see, you may actually lose money for a short period of time. You may have a great sauce for hot dogs, so you buy a little cart and go downtown, where a lot of people are walking between offices. People like your hot dogs and sauce, so they come back the next day. After three months, you set up four more carts at other busy street corners. Six months later, you package the concept and the system and begin selling the information. You become the "Subway of Hot Dogs" and make upward of a million dollars a year.

Example: Bill became a distributor for NASCAR model cars in 1993. He did not invent anything, patent anything, or manufacture a product. He simply distributes these toy cars to local toy stores and hobby shops. He had no guaranteed income or salary base. But with the growing popularity of NASCAR, today he grosses over $250,000 worth of product every month, with a net income of about $35,000 a month.

The loss of a paycheck may seem frightening and catastrophic, whether it occurs unexpectedly or as a result of your own choosing. Don't be intimidated by the thought of being paid for results rather than time. And don't immediately assume that your income will be reduced and your ability to give to others lessened. Once you see the power and the flexibility in the results-based way of earning a living, you will realize the possibilities for *in-*

creased income and control over your time. You'll find yourself more able to be involved in worthy causes, including your personal growth. The unwelcome loss of a job may be the key to unlocking pent-up creativity, imagination, and innovation. Expect nothing less.

If You're a Revolutionary, You Will

- Recognize that time doesn't always deserve compensation.
- Discover that results are what create income.
- Free yourself from a paycheck mentality.
- Understand that "security" comes from producing excellent results.
- Realize that not getting a paycheck may open the door to extraordinary income.

8

FINDING WORK THAT FITS

Aaron, a neighbor of mine out here in the rural area of Tennessee, is a young man who dropped out of school after the eighth grade and never got a high school diploma. As the oldest of six kids living with his divorced mom, he was angry about the burden he felt at such a young age.

With what seemed like limited options, he struggled with the question "What can I possibly do?" He worked in a variety of odd jobs, including hanging drywall. At age twenty-one he got married, and he and his wife quickly had two babies. Aaron was determined to make more money but saw few options other than working more hours. But he discovered that he was pretty good as a diagnostic mechanic, and he loved working on cars.

He started working on Saabs and Volvos. We live in Williamson County, Tennessee, just south of Nashville, and Aaron tells me there are more Volvos per capita in our county than in any other in the United States. He saw that as an opportunity and educated himself on those two makes of cars.

Aaron began working out of an old, deserted barn on the property where he and his growing family were living in a rented trailer. The first year, he did about $65,000 worth of mechanical work. The next year, he did $120,000. At that point, there was a lot of traffic in and out of that old barn, and that became an issue with the neighbors. So Aaron rented a warehouse in the nearby town of Franklin. His first year there he did $640,000 in business. Now it's two years later, and his projections for this year are $1.2 million in business revenue. (See http://www.eurofix online.com.)

Aaron didn't make it past the eighth grade but still discovered his niche. He found what fit him, which is a critical part of the process I've been describing. He didn't have the finances to start a business—most anyone would have advised him just to keep any possible job. But he was hungry enough that he didn't care about logical decisions. He says he started this business with a nineteen-dollar floor jack from Wal-Mart and a plastic toolbox with sixty dollars' worth of tools. Aaron told me, "The reason this work fits me is because it's fast paced and I like to fix people and their cars. I get to take their problems away. If I get to better someone's life and help my employees, then I'm happy, too."

Many people ask me, "Dan, where are the hottest opportunities? What are the best ideas to start?" Well, there are a lot of opportunities and ideas that excite *me*, but the key is to *find something that fits you*. Keep in mind, your heart has to be in sync with your mind for an idea to be successful. And your heart has to be attentive to your "vocation"—God's often quiet but ever-present voice, calling you to find the authentic fit where your work matches your talents.

Remember that most of this process is still looking inward. What are your unique gifts? What are you drawn to? What is it that you have enjoyed over the years? What are your recurring dreams? That's where you're likely to find your calling.

When people hear a story like Aaron's, they still frequently ask, "How do I get over my fear of stepping out on my own?" To answer, there are a couple of things that I want to restate from earlier chapters. First of all, branching out on your own is no riskier than working for a traditional company, where most of you do not have a whole lot of control over your salary or your security. However, if you jump on the first small business opportunity that comes your way or dive into a network marketing company that your friend tells you about without doing your research and understanding it well, you're putting yourself at risk. The more you research possible opportunities and plan things out, the more you reduce your risk.

> In the future, most people's jobs will involve scrambling around like frightened chipmunks trying to find the next paycheck in an endless string of unrelated short-term jobs. But since "Frightened Chipmunk" doesn't look very impressive on a business card, people will call themselves entrepreneurs, consultants, and independent contractors.
>
> —Scott Adams, *The Dilbert Future*

Ten Work Models

Here's a brief overview of ten new work models—from the very traditional to the very nontraditional. It will give you a sense of the wealth of opportunities available to you and, I hope, shed some light on what model fits you. Keep in mind that the descriptions are just examples; you can plug in many variations to each of the ten positions I describe. If you decide to remain an employee, you have simply chosen one work model. There's nothing wrong with that, but recognize it as only one of many choices available.

Here is an exercise that will help you determine whether a traditional job or a less conventional one would be a better fit for you. As you'll see, if you score a total of 6 points, or thereabouts, you are probably suited to find or keep a position as a traditional employee. If you score 40 points or higher, you are likely a candidate to move into nontraditional work. Either way, read on to see examples that fall in each of the ten categories. You may be surprised at which models you find attractive.

TRADITIONAL WORK		NONTRADITIONAL WORK
I prefer a more structured workday.	1 2 3 4 5 6 7 8 9 10	I like each day to be different.
I prefer a guaranteed paycheck each week.	1 2 3 4 5 6 7 8 9 10	I am willing to be compensated for my results rather than my time.
I prefer to have benefits paid for by my employer.	1 2 3 4 5 6 7 8 9 10	I am willing to provide my own benefits.
I am comfortable with earning a fixed income.	1 2 3 4 5 6 7 8 9 10	I would prefer no limits on the income I can earn.
I prefer to have decisions about salary, responsibilities, and work hours be made by my superiors.	1 2 3 4 5 6 7 8 9 10	I like to make all my own decisions about my work.
I prefer a set schedule, such as nine to five, five days a week.	1 2 3 4 5 6 7 8 9 10	I prefer to manage my own time.

1. Traditional Work

Show up at 7:30, punch the time clock, leave at 4:30. One-hour lunch break, paycheck every other Friday, two weeks' vacation, 401(k) retirement program, and medical insurance. Yes, this is still an option, but keep in mind, the opportunities for this kind of work are diminishing. Companies are looking for ways to avoid all of these predictable characteristics because they realize that guaranteeing income for time alone is a very dangerous business model. Ultimately, results have to be produced. Therefore, they are looking for ways to pay only for results. When any announcement is made about massive layoffs, company stocks soar. Shareholders recognize that the fixed expense of guaranteed wages and benefits is the biggest threat to bottom-line profitability.

> He who cannot obey himself will be commanded.
> This is the nature of living creatures.
> —Friedrich Nietzsche

As soon as you consider the possibility of other work models, you greatly increase your chances of finding or creating the work you love. I encourage you to recognize that you are working for yourself regardless of the model you choose. So if you enjoy the predictable structure of a traditional job, remember you can create that for yourself. In my own work, I am my harshest taskmaster. I have a clear schedule and set my own difficult deadlines. No one is looking over my shoulder. I know I'm responsible for the results, and I also know my rewards will be directly proportional to those results. You should expect to do the same, regardless of the work model you choose. Even if you work for someone else, you can take greater control over your schedule and ask to be compensated for the results you produce. The lines between these work models are soft and fluid, not hard and fast.

Is Traditional Work Right for You?

- Do you love getting to work each morning and seeing all your coworkers?
- Do you cringe at the thought of having to deal with your own taxes and financial paperwork?

2. Freelance Work

If you are a graphic artist, website designer, accountant, data management expert, sports trainer, or other such specialist, you may elect to find four or five companies that could use your services but are not large enough to employ you full-time. This way of working can be a tremendous advantage for both you and the companies who hire you. They get your expertise but don't have to find things for you to do forty hours a week. You have just increased your security by having four or five clients instead of one. If one company "fires" you, it will be necessary to replace only that 20 percent of your business, not the 100 percent that you'd have to replace after parting with a traditional job. As a freelancer, you can reasonably expect to triple your hourly income. Therefore, if you were making fifteen dollars an hour as a salaried graphic designer, you should expect to move up to forty-five. You can't expect to bill for forty hours a week, but perhaps twenty-five to thirty, still effectively doubling your income. Yes, you will have to allow for benefits that may not be provided. But there is nothing magical about benefits—they all translate into money. For example, just calculate the real value of your health insurance and build it into your plan. There are great insurance packages available for freelancers and the self-employed, some of which you can find at Internet sites like http://www.quote smith.com.

A couple of years ago I helped Monica, a graphic designer, do exactly what I just described. She actually went from $12.50 to $40.00 per hour, but quickly realized that was just a fraction of what she could be making. She began bidding her work by the project rather than by the hour and made over $100,000 the second year, doing primarily record label graphic design. She has three computers set up in her home, working the flexible time she desires as a single mom.

Under this arrangement, you may be called a freelance

worker, an independent contractor, a contingency worker, or a temp. The general rule is that an individual is considered an *independent contractor* if the person for whom the services are performed has the right to control or direct only the result of the work, and not what will be done and how.

Companies don't have to withhold federal, state, and Social Security (FICA) taxes, or pay unemployment or workers' compensation insurance for independent contractors. They also don't need to offer benefits like paid sick leave, vacation, health insurance, and stock options. Your willingness to take responsibility for those things can also remove the ceiling for your income potential.

Is Freelance Work Right for You?

- Do you feel like much of what you currently do is outside your strongest skill area?
- Would you be more energized by working with multiple companies but focusing on your area of expertise with each of them?

3. *Selling*

You are the Midwest representative for Nike. You operate within a clear corporate structure; however, you set your own schedule and are responsible for the results. You may have a base salary, but a large percentage of your income will be based on the sales you generate. You recognize that the more you move away from a traditional eight-to-five job, the more open-ended the income potential becomes.

Neal works for a large paper manufacturer and sells to printing companies in a small circle around his home in Brentwood, Tennessee. He loves calling on his friends, is home every night, and makes an annual income of about $160,000. Any company in existence needs productive salespeople. Just make sure there is a match in this work model with your strongest areas of competence.

Is Selling Right for You?

- Are you self-motivated—eager to get out each morning and make sales contacts?
- Are you excited about being paid according to your results rather than your time?

4. Consulting

You realize that you are knowledgeable about health and safety requirements in the workplace. So, rather than diluting your abilities in a traditional job, you decide to offer this one area of expertise to multiple companies. You charge eight thousand dollars a week but are responsible for booking yourself for these commitments. This is a model used by many people who, after years of working in the corporate environment, recognize they have a highly marketable area of expertise.

Revolutionary Insight

Can You Sell?

Recognize that lots of successful ideas are based on having great sales skills. Yes, I know, many people are intimidated by selling—because they're afraid of rejection or think they don't have the right personality to sell. But you can and *you must* sell. See the selling process as learning how to gain the trust of your customers, listening to their needs, and offering the right solutions.

No matter what you do, your marketing skills will account for 90 percent of your success. With nearly every new idea, people put too much emphasis on developing the product or idea and not enough on marketing. If you have a new invention, 2 percent of your challenge will be protecting your idea (with a patent, trademark, or copyright); 8 percent of your challenge will be determining whether it is a valid idea or product; and 90 percent of your challenge will be creating your marketing plan. Most people spend too much initial time, energy, and money protecting their idea rather than marketing it.

The dictionary defines a consultant as "an expert in a particular field who works as an advisor either to a company or to another individual." Well, that sounds pretty vague. And because of that vagueness, consultants have been the brunt of many jokes in corporate environments. You've certainly heard that a consultant is someone who borrows your watch, then tells you what time it is. Scott Adams, in his famous Dilbert writings, says, "A consultant is a person who takes your money and annoys your employees while tirelessly searching for ways to extend the consulting contract."[1] Of course, we know the unique value consultants can bring to an organization. They can be focused on limited areas of expertise and lend that specific knowledge to a company that would not be able to justify having the consultant retained as a full-time employee.

If done properly, the transition from being an employee to being a consultant is not a quantum leap. It's simply about defining a clear area of expertise and focusing on helping others with that area. Don't try to be a generalist. Be very specific about your competence. For example, if you have been the human resources person for a company, you may well be qualified to be an HR consultant. Do you know how many businesses there are that are not large enough to have a full-time HR staff person but could use your expertise one day a week, or need someone to put consistent practices in place for effective hiring?

Do you understand computers? Do you keep up with new software applications and changing technology? There are probably more computer consultants than any other area of specialty, and the opportunities are growing every day. Are you an expert in fund-raising? Do you like working with nonprofits? These are two growing areas of opportunity.

Some of the top areas for consulting today include:

- Accounting
- Marketing and advertising
- Small business

- Computer and communication technology
- Grant writing
- Human resources
- Payroll management
- Public relations

You may be brought in as a consultant to teach, to train, to advise, to identify problems, to supplement the existing staff, to do the dirty work of terminating someone, to hire new people, to help create a new division, to administer personality profiles, or to perform any of a host of other unique services.

While the rules regarding certification or licensing are vague, you may want to get certified by an organization that trains in your specialty. But I've found that most companies aren't as interested in certification as they are in who you are and what you've done. That may sound unsophisticated, but it's very much like the hiring process for employees. As much as we like to think degrees and certifications are the secret keys to success, we know that for many jobs that's not true. While some academic professions, of course, require specific degrees, most hiring decisions are made in the first three to five minutes of an interview, and they're not based on the list of degrees behind your name. They're made in response to questions the interviewer is asking himself or herself:

- Do I like this person?
- Is this person fun to be around?
- Will this person fit in as part of the team?

The same is true for consulting. No one will hire you unless they like you. As with any of the new work models, you must be able to sell yourself.

As a consultant, you no longer will have to perform a wide variety of tasks, many of which might not suit your talents. You can be very focused in what you do each day. You may not need an office; you may be able to do large parts of your work from your home, and you can work only with clients you enjoy.

Is Consulting Right for You?

- Do you have a clear area of expertise that brings people to seek out your advice?
- Do you have the maturity and contact base to launch yourself in this way?

PROFESSIONAL SPEAKING AND WRITING While professional speaking often falls in the category of consulting, I have broken it out here because I see it growing so dramatically. As corporations downsize, they eliminate many of their in-house specialists. But they are open to bringing in someone from the outside for a half day or so to present, teach, train, or motivate on a particular topic. I have many friends who make a very nice living traveling around speaking to companies. Their rates range from $1,500 to $35,000 a day. Obviously, some of them have discovered the power of having published books that add to their credibility. Even self-publishing your books can build your perceived value as a speaker. You can join an organization like the National Speakers Association (http://www.nsaspeaker .org) to connect with and learn from others who are making their living from speaking. You can get yourself listed with a speakers' bureau. But all successful speakers I know have very clear marketing plans in place and don't depend on a speakers' bureau.

Is Speaking Right for You?

- Are you frequently asked to present your ideas on a topic because people recognize you as an authority on that issue?
- Do you have a book idea you'd like to develop? My first published book grew out of a Sunday school class

when people kept asking for notes and outlines they could give to friends who needed to hear the message.

5. Franchising

The names are familiar: Wendy's, McDonald's, Chem-Dry, and Matco Tools. You happen to like sports, so you buy a Play It Again Sports franchise. You pay a franchise fee and a small monthly royalty, but in return you get a clear operating manual. You are your own boss but have a clear plan to follow. Not all franchises require $500,000 to start. There are legitimate franchises, like BuildingStars commercial cleaning or Jazzercise exercise classes, whose franchise fees can be from $2,000 to $3,000.

Jeff saw his job as a commercial airline pilot eliminated shortly after 9/11. He still loved travel but recognized that his position as a pilot had controlled his life and kept him from meaningful family events. He purchased a $10,000 cruise franchise and now books people on cruises from a closet work space in his house. He and his wife cruise several times a year—making money while spending quality time together. Franchising promotes the concept of being in business *for yourself, but not by yourself.*

Is Franchising Right for You?
- Do you enjoy daily contact with lots of people?
- Do you enjoy managing and motivating entry-level employees?

6. Distributorship

You find a product or service that you are excited about. You ask to be the area, state, or national distributor. You may sell the product and have it shipped from the company, simply collecting the difference between distributor and wholesale or retail prices. Distributorships do not require that you invent or manufacture anything; you simply distribute. Keep in mind, the distributors usually make more than those who manufacture or invent. At my company, we distribute books from several publishers because we can purchase them for 50 percent of the retail price. You can ask to be a distributor for most any product. Any manufacturer or publisher is looking for more ways to market and sell its products. If you have a simple resale license from your state, you will be welcomed by most as a legitimate distributor.

Susanne and Jimmy wanted to provide a small lock-box for parents who wanted to secure family prescriptions. They contacted a safe manufacturer, and now sell its product to families all over the world. They repurposed a common product and make extraordinary income for being able to see that new use.

Is a Distributorship Right for You?

- Is there a product or group of products that you believe in and would enjoy promoting to others?
- Are you part of an affinity group, a group that shares a common interest? Examples include Harley-Davidson motorcycle riders, golfers, tennis players, music lovers, and Corvette owners.

7. *Licensing*

You are a fan of country music. And you have a great idea for a T-shirt design showing Alan Jackson in his T-Bird. Now hold on a second. Before you launch your product, you have to negotiate a licensing agreement with Alan's people. But then you have the advantage of instant recognition; you go to the next concert and make twenty thousand dollars selling your shirts. Licensing is a great way to jump-start a business without having to build your marketing and reputation from zero. The most licensed entity in the world is NASCAR. But also look at the thousands of people who are making money with celebrity phrases like "You're fired"—that's another example of licensing.

Is Licensing Right for You?

- Can you imagine the possibilities of multiple ways of selling—in stores, on the Internet, at street festivals, and in catalogs?
- Does the idea of having your own product fulfillment center appeal to you?

8. *Business Opportunity*

While looking through a magazine, you see an ad for a system that gold-plates small objects. You realize all your motorcycle friends are constantly looking for new ways to customize their machines. You pay fifteen hundred dollars for an instruction manual and a tool that allows you to gold-plate any object smaller than twelve inches long. A business opportunity shows you a system that other people have used to run a successful business. Business opportunities are not regulated like franchises, so check them out carefully. But they also tend to be much less expensive to start and don't require you to pay royalties. You can find opportunities dealing with health issues, children's services, business needs, and sports and recreation interests. Many require an initial investment of less than a thousand dollars.

Is a Business Opportunity Right for You?

- Do you see interesting things you could do to make money when you are just driving down the street?
- Have you frequently thumbed through the back pages of magazines like *Entrepreneur* and *Business Start-Ups,* just to check out all the business ideas being promoted?
- Did you sell Girl Scout cookies or Christmas cards door to door as a child?

9. Personal Service

You buy a lawn mower for $138. That afternoon, you go out and offer to mow your neighbor's yard for sixty dollars a week. When you have booked your weekly schedule, you hire your nephew to work for you at ten dollars an hour. You duplicate this model and one year later have fifty residential and fourteen commercial accounts for year-round yard maintenance. So many ideas fall in the category of personal service. (For instance, my family lives in the country, and we have a well. I've always wished someone would come by once a month and check our well's filters and salt levels.) If you can wash windows, build gazebos, do personal training or massage, shop for the elderly, or do housecleaning, you can start today with your own venture. It's just a matter of thinking about what kinds of services people need and deciding whether you can provide them.

Is a Personal Service Right for You?

- Do you have an ability or area of expertise that you are convinced plenty of potential customers would pay for? Remember, what seems common to you may be a valuable skill to someone else.
- Would you rather have fifteen customers than work for one company? And have the possibility of making significantly more income?

10. "I Never Thought of That!" Work

As a fabric sales representative, Chuck realized the local apparel factories would reject entire rolls of fabric because of the smallest flaw. He began purchasing the fabric as scrap for pennies on the original cost. He and his wife then cut it into small squares that they began to sell as cleanup rags to auto dealerships, body shops, and retail outlets. After ninety days, Chuck received a contract with Dollar General to supply these rags, packaged in colorful plastic bags. The first year, Chuck and his wife netted $150,000 working on their own schedule from their garage.

There are so many ways to make treasure out of other people's trash. I always cringe when I hear about someone who has been looking for work for fourteen months—with no income during that time. It seems to me there are opportunities all around, even if it's not the perfect job or business. I have an enormous pile of wood chips, mainly cedar, on my rural property. They make a soft, aromatic, and beautifully red-tinted cushion for our walking trails. They could also be used in children's playground areas, around shrubs and trees, in patio areas, et cetera. People would pay premium dollars for this upscale mulch. Guess what I paid for this wealth of material? Zero. We befriended a couple of tree-trimming companies in the area, and they are delighted to have a place to dump their waste without having to drive way out to the landfill. Their waste is our bonus. I know without a doubt this pile could be turned into a profitable business if I chose to do so.

Bob and Carol visit a clothing liquidation center every Monday morning. They buy brand-name clothing at about ten cents on the dollar. They then place those items on eBay and consistently triple their money. Their children help them package and ship out of their garage. Bob has doubled his previous income as a salesman who was on the road from Monday through Friday, and he gets to spend more time with his family.

Is "I Never Thought of That!" Work Right for You?

- Are you good at seeing new opportunities that others miss?
- Have you always thought eventually you would have your own business?

Each of these work models can be put into practice in scores of ways. But you get the idea of the choices available, from those structured by external forces to those that allow you to be completely independent. It is not a black-and-white issue of either working for someone else or working for yourself. You can take graduated moves away from the traditional job, or you may be able to find a place on that continuum that fits exactly what you are looking for. Also, as you recognize all the options, you can see that it may not involve a big leap to go from what you are currently doing to a new model that fits you and allows you to reach your goals.

The real point here is that, as a Revolutionary, you recognize all the work models that are available. So often I encounter peo-

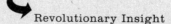

Revolutionary Insight

What Is Your Dream?

I had the privilege of interviewing Jim Hodges for a teleseminar titled *30-Second Commute: Working from Home.* Jim reads history books, producing audio recordings that make history come alive for students young and old. He travels to home-schooling conferences and other educational events to share his products. And now book publishers are coming to ask him to produce their audio recordings. So how did Jim find this line of work? Several years ago, while they were out on a dinner date, Jim's wife asked him, "If you could do whatever you wanted to, what would that be?" Jim immediately replied, "I'd read history books."

So how do you take that kind of dream and turn it into a real, income-producing outcome? Most people would have finished dinner and gone back to the drudgery of real life. However, with Jim, the seed was somehow planted.

In submitting his work description to me, Jim said, "Honestly, I never work anymore. The entire business, from recording to marketing to traveling to conventions, all of it, is immensely pleasurable for me." (You can listen to a sample of Jim's enthusiastic reading at http://www.hentybooksontape.com.)

What could you do if you acted on your real dreams rather than squashing them?

ple who are wringing their hands because no one will hire them. If you have clearly identifiable areas of competence, companies should be happy to consider bringing you on their teams. But once you identify those areas of competence, you don't have to wait on a company to hire you because you'll see many opportunities for the application of your skills—getting a job would be just one of many choices. However, if you can't identify your areas of competence, why would anyone want to hire you anyway?

The power which resides in him is new in nature, and none but he knows what that is, which he can do, nor does he know until he's tried.

—Ralph Waldo Emerson

Don't Let a Search for "Security" Lead You into a Trap!

One day, while soaring through the sky, the Chicken said to his good friend the Eagle: "Let's drop down and get a bite to eat. My stomach is growling." "Sounds like a good idea to me," replied the Eagle. So the two birds glided down to earth, saw several animals eating, and decided to join them. The Cow was busy eating corn, but upon noticing that the Eagle and the Chicken were sitting on the ground next to her, she said, "Welcome. Help yourself to the corn."

This took the two birds by surprise. They were not accustomed to having other animals share their food quite so readily. "Why are you willing to share your corn with us?" asked the Eagle. "Oh, we have plenty to eat here. Mr. Farmer gives us all we want," replied the Cow. With that invitation, the Eagle and the Chicken jumped in and ate their fill. When they finished, the Chicken asked more about Mr. Farmer. "Well," said the Cow, "he grows all our food. We don't have to work for the food at all."

"You mean," said the Chicken, "that Mr. Farmer simply gives you all you want to eat?" "That's right," said the Cow. "Not only that, but he gives us a place to live." The Chicken and the Eagle were shocked! They had always had to search for food and work for shelter.

When it came time to leave, the Chicken and the Eagle began to discuss the situation. "Maybe we should just stay here," said the Chicken. "We can have all the food we want without working. And that barn over there sure beats those nests we have been building. Besides, I'm getting tired of always having to work for a living."

"I don't know about all this," said the Eagle. "It sounds too good to be true. I find it hard to believe that one can get something for nothing. Besides, I kinda like flying high and free through the air. And providing for food and shelter isn't so bad. In fact, I find it quite challenging."

The Eagle flew back to his natural environment while the Chicken stayed on the farm, where food and shelter were free. Everything went fine for the Chicken. He ate all he wanted. He never worked. But then one day he heard the farmer say to his wife that the preacher was coming to visit the next day and they should have fried chicken for dinner. Hearing that, the Chicken decided it was time to check out and rejoin his good friend Mr. Eagle. But when he attempted to fly, he found that he had grown too fat and lazy to get off the ground. Instead of being able to fly, he could only flutter. So the next day the farmer's family and the preacher sat down to a lovely meal of fried Chicken.

When you give up the challenges of life in pursuit of security, you may also give up your freedom. Has the temptation of security led you into a potential trap in your own life?

For many people, the prospect of leaving a traditional employee position conjures up the thought of having to become a hard-driving, egotistical, obnoxious Donald Trump or Ted Turner. The expectation is that any work venture done independently requires dominant, aggressive personal characteristics. People who may be more introverted, analytical, and methodical suspect that there are no fitting opportunities for them outside of working for a company. I intend to convince you how erroneous that thinking is. With the explosion of ideas utilizing information, service, and technology, it is not a requirement that any one set of personality traits be present. The new work models can be designed to fit whatever skills you bring to the table. Sales and marketing systems can be created in ways that bypass any need for nose-to-nose selling, thereby allowing positioning for those people who will never have the Donald's flair or arrogance.

Entrepreneur versus Eaglepreneur

Perhaps a helpful clarification is the distinction between the typical entrepreneur and what I call the Eaglepreneur. Many people who want to break off on their own are intimidated by the seemingly endless licenses, forms, tax codes, et cetera, that are presented as part of starting any business. Then there are the lease negotiations, the sign permits, the hiring of employees, and the bank loans or other means of raising money. These may be undesirable components of what you thought you wanted. And yet you are intrigued by, and attracted to, the time flexibility, the personal freedom, and the open-ended income potential possible when you have your own venture.

Today's new Revolutionaries are often graphic designers, accountants, video producers, computer consultants, writers, inventors, public relations specialists, sales and marketing professionals, direct mail masters, caterers, and designers. Others are personal service providers who specialize in pet sitting, care for the elderly, painting, or landscape services. They may not want to run a traditional business with a building, leases, loans, and employees. Be encouraged if you are one of these new entrepreneurs. You may in fact be an Eaglepreneur.

The Small Business Administration defines a small business as any organization with one hundred to fifteen hundred em-

ployees.[2] In all practical applications, what is required to run a
one- or two-person venture is obviously substantially different
from what is required to run even a ten-person company. Unfortunately, most of the courses offered, and the books available,
deal with the traditional small business of one hundred to fifteen
hundred employees. If you are an Eaglepreneur, the dynamics of
what you will be doing will not just be a scaled down version of
that kind of business. They will be dramatically different. Trying
to run your business like a bigger business is comparable to trying to buy a Ferrari when you need a Volkswagen. There is no
need to make your venture more complicated than it has to be.
If you have been a professional and want to go out on your own,
it probably will not take a quantum leap to make the transition.

We all know about the big companies like Wal-Mart,
Microsoft, Dell computers, and General Motors, with their thousands of employees and buildings that would make a small city.
But it's interesting to look at how rare that kind of business
model is today. According to the Bureau of Labor Statistics, here
are the real figures for business size in America:[3]

52.8 percent of all businesses have 1–4 employees.
97.4 percent of all businesses have 1–99 employees.

Which means that only 2.6 percent of all businesses have more
than 99 employees, and a tiny percentage of those actually fit the
Small Business Administration definition of a small business.

We are in a culture that recognizes big business. We hear that
AT&T is laying off 40,000 workers and that the stock of Columbia/
HCA is falling. We see the collapse of Enron and WorldCom and
become convinced that there will be no jobs left anywhere. We
hear the new figures about foreign outsourcing of even more
jobs, and the panic increases. The Detroit automakers announce
that they will be cutting 100,000 positions over the next couple
of years. Economic reports tell us that over 1 million jobs are being eliminated each year by big business. What we do not hear

about as much is that in each of the last few years small, independent ventures created over 2 million new positions. The
heartbeat of the emerging American workforce is not being created in the factories and monolithic institutions; it is being created out in the streets and in the homes of America's new
entrepreneurs and Eaglepreneurs.

Look at the following comparisons:

ENTREPRENEUR	EAGLEPRENEUR
1. Finds a need and fills it	1. Anticipates or creates a need
2. Rents or leases offices	2. May work from home with no office
3. May need $500,000 to $1 million in capital	3. May start with no capital; uses time, energy, and imagination, often no $.*
4. Hires employees	4. Often has no employees**
5. Is product focused	5. Is service or information focused
6. Is interested in *running* the business	6. Is interested in *doing* the business
7. Wants to work *on* the business	7. Wants to work *in* the business
8. Focuses on *big* business	8. Focuses on *small* business
9. Builds and starts expanding	9. Builds and then maintains a clear focus
10. Is driven by *profits*	10. Is driven by *purpose*
11. Measures sales, money as gauge of success	11. Measures relationships as gauge of success
12. Keeps eye peeled for competitors to eliminate	12. Looks for companies to cooperate with
13. Is oriented toward *taking:* How much can we take from our customers?	13. Is oriented toward *giving:* What can we give our customers?
14. May build the business and sell it	14. Would continue after winning the lottery
15. Spends time managing	15. Spends time creating
16. May have had many businesses	16. May have been a loyal employee

According to the Census Bureau, 60 percent of businesses being started today require less than $5,000. Twenty-six percent of all business start-ups don't require any capital. Yet the common myth continues that you need a ton of money to start a profitable business. Many people also believe that there is a correlation between how much money is required initially and how much money the business can make. Not true! There are people borrowing $500,000 to open a bowling alley, a traditional business, who will work sixty-five hours a week and net $35,000 a year. Someone else may spend $300 to open a site on the Internet, spend a couple hours a day updating its information, and net $150,000 the first year.

**Don't think that, just because you have no employees, you cannot benefit from the efforts of a lot of people. Franchises, business opportunities, and strategic alliances are all common ways people can leverage their time and benefit from the efforts of others. Many people are attracted to network marketing because they have been told that is the only way to get a small part of the efforts of a lot of people. There is an old J. Paul Getty principle that says, "I would rather have 1 percent of the efforts of one hundred people than 100 percent of my own." That is a valid principle, but network marketing is only one of many ways to accomplish that goal. And that work model is not a style fit for many people. Much of the power of a business is starting with a work model that fits you.*

Education makes people easy to lead, but difficult to drive; easy to govern, but impossible to enslave.

—Henry Peter Brougham

Change or Die?

A study from the medical field reported in *Fast Company*[4] presents some startling theories about how we change—or rather resist change. The study shows that 90 percent of the patients who have heart surgery and know they could avoid returning pain and surgery if they changed to a healthier lifestyle don't do anything.

Here are the findings:

- Crisis is not a powerful motivator for change.
- Change is not motivated by fear.
- Knowing the facts does not cause us to change.
- It's easier to make drastic changes than to make small ones.

For years I have scratched my head at the people who hate their jobs but do nothing. Or those who, even when it's obvious the company is closing, freeze like a deer in the headlights. Why is it often only upon being fired that they take any action? After all, the study highlights that the "joy of living" is a stronger motivator than the "fear of dying."

Having the expectation that you're really moving to work you love is likely going to be a stronger motivator than just knowing you hate your current position. I've always emphasized the importance of seeing what you're *going to* over knowing what you're *going from*. Here's an important point. If your current daily actions are not moving you *toward* your goals, then you are probably moving *away from* your goals. Our daily actions are never neutral. What are you doing now that is moving you toward the

....

POT-SHOTS
Brilliant Thoughts in 17 Words or Less

©ASHLEIGH BRILLIANT 1992

What I need
is
a job I can
get
without ever
having to
make a good
impression.

Ashleigh Brilliant
SANTA BARBARA

POT-SHOTS NO. 5690.

things you want to accomplish in life, toward becoming the person you want to be, toward fulfilling the ultimate purpose for your life? What actions are actually moving you away from your goals and your purpose? Everything counts—either for or against your desired direction. And the research shows that, most of the time, it's better to create a radical change than just attempt tiny adjustments. Hey, moving to Tahiti to open that windsurfing shop may be the best path to your success after all. Commit to radical change to improve your life!

Self-Employed or Business Owner?

I frequently ask readers of my weekly newsletter to submit business plans for their ideas. Here's an observation: About 80 percent of the ideas submitted would move that person from being an employee to being self-employed but would not really result in a business. The difference can be determined easily: Does any income continue to be generated when the owner is on vacation or at home asleep? Neither is right or wrong; just be sure you recognize the distinctions.

There are four primary options for generating income: employee, self-employed, business owner, and investor. If you want to do independent accounting, financial consulting, graphic design, or lawn mowing, you may be looking at being self-employed. Those are likely examples of being an Eaglepreneur as opposed to an entrepreneur. An Eaglepreneur is someone who just wants to work on his or her own. That is actually the model most appealing to me. But having a *business* implies that there are systems in place that would create income even if you are not there. If you want a business, make sure you are really developing systems that will work for you. If you are self-employed, you will likely be limited by the number of hours in a day and the number of days in a week. In order to break out of those limitations, you will have to develop relationships or

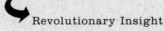

Revolutionary Insight

We Hear What We Listen For

Two men were walking along a crowded sidewalk in a downtown business area. Suddenly one exclaimed: "Listen to the lovely sound of that cricket." But the other could not hear. He asked his companion how he could detect the sound of a cricket amid the din of people and traffic. The first man, who was a zoologist, had trained himself to listen to the voices of nature. But he didn't explain. He simply took a coin out of his pocket and dropped it to the sidewalk, whereupon a dozen people began to look about them. "We hear," he said, "what we listen for."

—Kermit L. Long[5]

processes to allow your income flow to continue 168 hours a week. The goal is not to have to work 80 hours a week to create reasonable income—rather, the goal is to develop systems to reduce the time required while the income potential increases anyway.

Many people leave employee positions only to discover that all they did was create or even purchase another job for themselves. There is a clear distinction there. Personally, I'm pretty fond of SWISS (Sales While I Sleep Soundly) dollars. Check your idea; see if it will help you get those SWISS dollars coming into your account.

Feeling Inadequate? Try This

It's important to have another reminder about the building blocks for choosing meaningful and fulfilling work. As you look at the many options, remember to be clear that this is a very individualized process. No matter how financially appealing or exciting an opportunity may appear, it must be an authentic *fit* that matches your (1) skills and abilities, (2) personality traits, and (3) values, dreams, and passions. Following your calling is a critical element and may take you in a direction that others would question. As you pray for spiritual insight, expect that the path that fulfills your unique calling will almost certainly embrace what you already know about yourself. God's intent is not to keep you in the dark: He provides lots of clues along the way. The more life experience you have, the clearer your own purpose should become.

> We must not conceive of prayer as an overcoming of God's reluctance, but as a laying hold of His highest willingness.
>
> —Richard Chenevix Trench

My son Jared has been living in Rwanda for some time now. He heads up an organization designed to bring a better way of living to those struggling most in that poverty-stricken nation. As a symbol of hope, the organization's projects provide jobs, transportation, and related microenterprises to further the economic and social development of that country.

In a note to our family the week before he left on his first trip to Rwanda, Jared said this:

> I am a bit intimidated by the magnitude of this project, and the possibility of it affecting so many lives, but I'm equally excited and I know I have the passion and determination to see it through, even if I am shaking in my boots. My passion for these people always exceeds my fears of inadequacy. In realizing that, I regain the confidence I need. [See http://www.sistersof rwanda.org.]

Now there's a key for overcoming the fears of inadequacy. *My passion exceeds my fears.* Staying true to your calling will release a passion for what you are doing; that will in turn override your fears of inadequacy.

Work at what you love. You'll never work more willingly, passionately, and fearlessly than when you work in line with your passion—where your *life will speak.* The extra boost of enthusiasm and energy generated by a clear passion will propel you to a level of success unattainable with any other motivation. If fear is crippling or limiting you, perhaps you are trying to do work that is not your passion. Working with raw ability alone is ultimately not enough to keep you going.

Joanne and I have our parental concerns about Jared going to Rwanda. But far be it from me to thwart him from the expression of his unique, compassionate dreams. With what I teach, how could I do anything but support him? His success will undoubtedly be realized most completely in pursuing his passion.

Are you working where you are most passionate?

If You're a Revolutionary, You Will

- Recognize the many options for choosing your own work model.
- See varied ways your areas of competence could be put to use.
- Explore being an Eaglepreneur.
- Choose what you are *going to* rather than just what you are leaving.
- Understand that fitting into God's perfect plan will embrace what you already know about yourself.
- Know that your passion will overcome your fears of inadequacy.

9

ONE PLACE FOREVER—
BLESSING OR CURSE?

I'll Drink to That . . .

You may have heard the old folktale about the village that was planning a grand New Year's Eve celebration. Every member of the village was asked to contribute a bottle of wine—and to make things easy, they would just pour the wine into one big barrel in the middle of town. At midnight, everyone would share a drink to usher in the new year.

On the special day, people came from all parts of town and emptied their personal bottles into the common barrel. At midnight, the town fathers opened the spigots and invited the people to celebrate the new year together. But unfortunately, when they raised their glasses, each person found not wine but water. Apparently, everyone in town had the same idea: *If all my neighbors bring great wine, no one will notice if I just slip in a bottle of water. The little bit of deception on my part won't be enough to spoil everyone's fun.*

I see this perspective played out in many work situations by people who believe a little cheating surely won't make a big difference. But what if that person slacking off was supposed to have installed a bolt in the steering mechanism of the new car you're driving on your family vacation? What if the Arthur Andersen employee thinks since everyone else is making the numbers work surely a little "creative accounting" on his or her part won't really make any difference? What if the trucker hauling milk doesn't properly clean out the liquid fertilizer he transported on the first leg of his trip, thinking a little bit of contamination won't matter?

By now, you've gotten a sense of how the new models of work can drastically reduce the time you spend working while increasing your income, personal freedom, and sense of fulfillment. But don't think they allow any room for cutting corners, slacking off, or getting others to do your work for you. If you don't take responsibility for finding and creating fulfilling work for yourself, who will? Revolutionaries are committed to their callings and expect the same of others, whereas liars, cheaters, and slackers hope that they are the only ones clever enough to get by with their schemes. Meaningful, purposeful work always translates into value for both you and those around you. The first person to be cheated by unethical shortcuts will be you.

When I was a little boy, my godly mother used to delight in singing this little poem: "What kind of world would this world be, if everyone in it were just like me?" I don't know the author, but the thought has returned to me throughout my life. Would you want everyone at your office to do what you did today? Would you want everyone in your house to act like you did today?

In this chapter I will address five of the most common questions regarding moving away from the traditional model of work. Many of them boil down to one common fear: Am I really capable of taking responsibility for my own career? My answer is: Not only *can* you, but you absolutely must! In our culture, we have an insidious expectation that someone other than ourselves is going to take responsibility for our future. We are now seeing fourth and fifth generations who rely on government welfare for a meager subsistence living and believe they have no other choice. We have seen thousands who expected their companies to provide health insurance and retirement programs only to learn the hard way that this wouldn't happen. Many already in retirement are dependent on a Social Security system that is rapidly becoming bankrupt. All of these people have been lulled into a dangerous complacency. The only person responsible for your career path and your financial future is the one you see in the mirror each morning.

Struggle Is a Necessary Part of Growth

A man found a cocoon of a butterfly. One day a small opening appeared. He sat and watched the butterfly for several hours as it struggled to force its body through that little hole. Then it seemed to stop making any progress. It appeared as if it had gotten as far as it could go—and it could go no farther. So the man decided to help the butterfly. He took a pair of scissors and snipped off the remaining bit of the cocoon. The butterfly then emerged easily, but it had a swollen body and small, shriveled wings.

The man continued to watch the butterfly because he expected that, at any moment, the wings would expand and gain the ability to support the body, which would contract. But neither happened! In fact, the butterfly spent the rest of its life crawling around with a swollen body and shriveled wings. It never was able to fly.

How do you view the struggles in your life? Do you do whatever you can to avoid them? Or do you see them as necessary steps for growth? Do you suspect evil forces are bombarding you? Or could it be that God is allowing the struggles to bring about your transformation—to allow the beautiful butterfly inside you to emerge? So, is getting fired a horrible disaster? Is failing in a business reason never to try that again? If I can't pay my electric bill, should I expect my church to take care of it for me?

And when your loved ones experience struggles, do you help them see the lesson in their troubles or do you attempt to find a quick fix for the problem? If your child has used up all his allowance and asks for more money to go to the movie with friends, what is the most growth-producing response? If a young couple purchased an expensive car and now cannot make the payments, what is the most helpful response?

> I don't want to get to the end of my life and find that
> I just lived the length of it. I want to have lived the
> width of it as well.
>
> —Diane Ackerman

Olympians and professional athletes go through years of rigorous daily training before they can ever expect to be competitive. Professional musicians spend hour upon hour making mistakes before finding the right notes for their symphonies. Do you recognize the valuable training that comes from the struggles in our daily lives?

The Tartar tribes of central Asia understood this reality when creating the powerful curse they used against their enemies. It was not that their houses would burn or that pestilence would befall them. Instead, the Tartars would say, "May you stay in one place forever." It might sound innocent enough at first, but think about the boredom and frustration that would soon result from such stagnation. If we don't see the maturing value of our struggles, that could be exactly our fate. Perhaps you've confused staying in one place with loyalty, persistence, or even security. Make sure it's not a camouflaged curse.

> Some defeats are only installments on the
> road to victory.

Can you recall a time when you yearned for relief from a tough situation? Did the struggle teach you something important? And what about now? Is losing a job or dealing with the pressures of a business limiting your opportunities—or preparing you for a burst of new success? Perhaps you're in the process of entering a new chapter of your life. Don't sabotage the growth process with a Band-Aid solution!

Five Revolutionary Work Questions

Whether you are thinking about launching a nontraditional career, staying in your current job, or exploring a hybrid of the two, the following questions are crucial to consider. It doesn't matter if you choose to be a freelance worker, a consultant, an independent contractor, a small business owner, or an employee; considering these questions will make you a lot less vulnerable—and perhaps a lot more valuable.

1. *I'm curious about a freelance or nontraditional career, but I crave the structure that comes from a nine-to-five job. Does that mean I'm doomed?*

If you need someone to tell you when to get up, when to show up at work, and when your paycheck is coming, then you need to stay in a traditional employee position. And there will always be opportunities in traditional work environments. Just recognize that you have looked at other options and made the choice to stay in a traditional job. But if you are self-motivated and willing to recognize you are responsible for the results you create, not just the time you put in, new opportunities are waiting for you. You can take a fresh look at your unique talents and passions, create a clear focus based on what you love doing, and translate that into meaningful, productive, and profitable work.

2. *I want to branch out on my own, but I've heard that most new ventures fail. What should I do?*

Currently, the National Federation of Independent Business is conducting research that helps us understand the information about businesses staying in business. In fact, because many entrepreneurs love the thrill of the launch, they simply choose to close a business, even a successful one, and go on to a new one. That does not mean the old business was not successful or even profitable; the entrepreneur just was ready for a new venture.

Here's an example of how this works. Michael started a land-scaping business in Franklin, Tennessee. The business grew quickly and added workers to keep up with the demand. However, after two years I sat down with Michael and looked at the patterns in his business growth. Although gross revenues had grown dramatically, his margins had not changed, and the addition of six-teen workers brought on new and challenging responsibilities. In doing his own research, Michael saw that approximately 70 percent of his high-income customers were prospects for some kind of water fountain in their yard. He also recognized that landscaping and lawn maintenance is an easy-entry business and eight new competitors had entered his market area. Michael redirected his business, keeping six of his most competent workers and changing his focus to the highly profitable water fountain business. He officially closed The Cutting Edge and opened under the name Scenic WaterWorks. If you analyzed business data, The Cutting Edge would show up as a business that didn't survive the first five years of operation. But you see what happened to Michael. He's a happy camper—not someone who failed but someone who refined his original idea and went on to even greater success.

3. *I've got a revolutionary idea. What next?*

According to the business trainer Brian Tracy, there are two primary reasons new ventures fail:

1. Lack of sales and marketing: 48 percent
2. Poor cost controls: 46 percent

Having a great product or service is not sufficient for business success. I can't emphasize this point enough. You must have a sales and marketing plan in place as well as a system to help you manage your money. Without them, failure is certain. Business ideas succeed for the same reasons you succeed in any area of your life. If you want to lose weight, you can't just look at magazines showing pictures of vegetables and exercise equipment.

You have to go beyond the idea and the desire and back them up with a concrete plan for eating great food and exercising four to five times a week. You need an equally clear plan for success in any business.

I see too many people who assume that a business that is small, or an extension of their hobby, doesn't require real business principles. Be diligent about your approach to managing and marketing your own work, and you can experience success in time freedom, satisfaction, and income. You may be the greatest artist in the world, or a wonderful sculptor, songwriter, or gifted interior designer; however, if you don't market aggressively, you will never experience professional or financial success. Mark Victor Hansen (cocreator of the Chicken Soup for the Soul series) told me once that he tells authors, "Write your book; now you're 10 percent finished. Ninety percent is the marketing—who will buy it, how can I price it, how can I get media attention, et cetera." Even as a writer, an artist, or a musician, you must understand sales and marketing issues or you will be broke and hungry.

> *A pile of rocks ceases to be a rock pile when someone contemplates it with the idea of a cathedral in mind.*
>
> —Antoine de Saint-Exupéry

4. But what if I don't know how to sell?

Everyone can sell. In fact, you can't afford not to! Where there is no ability to sell, even the finest product or service will fail. Selling may involve a passive method of marketing or a discreet way of talking up your venture, but someone must be selling in one form or another. Still worried you can't do it? Understand its importance and match your selling system to your personality. People typically think of the slick-haired, shiny-shoed cliché of the used car salesman, but that's a very narrow stereotype. Remember that the last time you bought groceries or gas, signed on to a

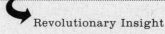

Revolutionary Insight

Boring Can Be Brilliant

Selling secondhand furniture back to the general public might not sound like a truly original business idea these days. But for Terri Bowersock of Arizona, the idea's been a serious money spinner for more than twenty years.[1] Terri borrowed $2,000 from her grandmother to set up Terri's Con-sign and Design Furnishings Store, stocking it entirely with her mother's living room furniture and her own bedroom furniture. Two weeks went by before she made her first sale, but after two years sales were at $4,000 a month. Today Terri has seven stores in the Phoenix area, as well as six ad-ditional franchised stores. The company now has 167 employees and an-nual revenues of $16 million.

It doesn't have to be rocket science—just an idea with a clear plan behind it.

new phone service, chose a vacation destination, decided on a church to attend, or even just picked a restaurant, someone was selling you that idea. There are many ways to sell. I write articles and books as the primary selling technique for my business. I might not pick up the phone or knock on anyone's door, but I am always selling. You may choose to use print or Internet ads, or the services of someone who sells better than you, but you will need a clear marketing plan in place. Without selling, the best product or service will languish.

5. If I leave my traditional job, who will provide my benefits?

There is nothing magical about the benefits you may now have or had in a previous employee position. They all translate into money. So if you had a transportation allowance, you can calculate how much that added to your income each month. If you had a 401(k) retirement contribution, simply determine how much additional money you would have to make to duplicate that benefit. Obviously, the big issue today is health insurance.

Revolutionary Insight

Rent a Cow

Today, cheese lovers can rent their very own cheesemaker—a brown-and-white cow living on a Swiss mountain.[2] Paul Wyler, who along with his wife, Helga, runs a fifty-head dairy farm in the Brienz area of the Bernese Oberland, offers his cows for rent on the Internet. Cows cost around $280 for the summer. Renters can check photographs of the cows at Wyler's website before they pay up. Paul and Helga look after the animals, make cheese from their milk, and send all that's produced to the "owners." They already rent some of the cows to restaurants, and say they came up with their rent-a-cow idea because they could not sell as much cheese as they produced every year. (See http://www.kuhleasing.ch.)

Now there's a unique idea. Take what you already have and what may actually be giving you a problem (in the Wylers' case, too much cheese) and create a novel and attention-getting solution. You don't need much aggressive selling when you have an interesting product or service.

But look at what is happening with that "benefit." Many companies are saying they will no longer absorb the rising costs of health insurance; others may elect to make only a small, set contribution.

If you have a health club allowance, calculate how much it costs and determine to make that much more on your own. If you got three weeks' vacation last year, plan how you could take four next year. If you get reimbursed for dry cleaning, think about how much you'll save by working in your blue jeans.

I like to be optimistic and see the bright side of the workplace. But the demise of pension plans is an issue that keeps raising its ugly head. As I mentioned earlier, the status of most employee pension plans sits somewhere between threatened, and dead and gone.

But there actually is a bright side—if only because it wakes us up to the fact that no company or government entity can guarantee us paychecks, insurance, or other benefits. As soon as you accept that, you will see amazing opportunities open up all around you. I have seen people stay in thirty-thousand-dollar-a-year positions to keep health insurance while passing up opportunities to make sixty thousand dollars on their own. Now you and I both know it doesn't require thirty thousand dollars a year to have health insurance. Health savings accounts (HSAs) offer a tax incentive for independent workers. Insurance companies know independent workers are less risky as clients than employees, and they are very competitive in seeking your business. You'll find that as an independent worker you are no longer limited by what one company can offer you. And you'll quickly realize why insurance companies compete to insure those who have left a traditional corporate environment. If a salary is in place, sick days are accumulating, and work is boring, what does an employee do about a nagging headache early in the morning? Doctors' visits are covered, sick days are longing to be used—why not take the day off, run by the clinic in the morning, and then enjoy the rest of the day? What does a free agent do when waking up with the same elusive malady? He's already found fulfilling work that he's eager to begin, if he's productive today his income goes up immediately, and he has a deductible on his insurance that would come right out of his pocket. So he shakes off the headache, jumps into his work, and by 10:00 A.M. totally forgets he wasn't feeling well. Welcome to the exciting world of *No More Dreaded Mondays*!

> *When one door closes another door opens; but we so often look so long and so regretfully upon the closed door, that we do not see the ones which open for us.*
>
> —Alexander Graham Bell

Revolutionary Insight

I'll Take One of Those . . .

It's true that you only need one good idea to make your fortune. Consider the California salesman Gary Dahl, who in 1975 came up with the idea for a Pet Rock, then took the idea a step further and decided to market a book giving instructions on how to care for the Pet Rock.

The fad for Pet Rocks spread like wildfire. Here was a pet that took no care and still gave its owner a few moments of pleasure. Unbelievably, a million rocks sold for $3.95 apiece in just a few months, and Gary Dahl—who decided from the beginning to make at least one dollar from every rock—had become a millionaire.

Now, stories like Gary's might be one in a million, but there's no reason why one good idea couldn't truly change your life—for the better!

Just Leave Me Alone

A common myth I hear among clients is that if they are going to do something creative, innovative, or entrepreneurial, they must become outgoing and aggressive—like the fast-talking blue-suede-shoe car salesman—even when this image runs counter to their natural personality style. But is it necessary to become the aggressive extrovert in order to do something exciting, unusual, and profitable?

I trust you don't really believe that. The key to success is to be true to who you really are. Shakespeare was onto a basic truth when he said, "This above all: to thine own self be true, and it must follow, as the night the day, thou canst not then be false to any man." If you are an introvert who shudders at the thought of standing in front of a crowd, then allow your business or career to honor that. A person needn't become more extroverted, talkative, bold, and aggressive in order to become more successful, healthy, or mature.

Here are some notable, quotable examples about the power of introversion from people whose success we all recognize:

Solitude is for me a fount of healing which makes my life worth living. Talking is often torment for me, and I need many days of silence to recover from the futility of words.

—Carl Jung

I hate crowds and making speeches. I hate facing cameras and having to answer to a crossfire of questions. Why popular fancy should seize upon me, a scientist, dealing in abstract things and happy if left alone, is a manifestation of mass psychology that is beyond me.

—Albert Einstein

We have to remember that we look for solitude in order to grow there in love for God and in love for others. We do not go into the desert to escape people but to learn how to find them: we do not leave them in order to have nothing more to do with them, but to find out the way to do them the most good.

—Thomas Merton

Or you may even take comfort in this Biblical directive:

When words are many, sin is not absent, but he who holds his tongue is wise.

—Proverbs 10:19 (NIV)

If You're a Revolutionary, You Will
- Work as hard as you would want everyone else to.
- View struggles as part of a healthy birthing process for a new season in your life.
- See "failure" differently than those around you.
- Research, plan, and organize around your idea.
- Be confident there are wildly successful ideas that match your unique talents and passions.

10

THROW OUT YOUR TV (AND YOUR ALARM CLOCK TOO!)

Every man takes the limits of his field of vision for the limits of the world.

—Arthur Schopenhauer

Should Have Known Better

In his first semester in college, Michael Dell started buying outmoded IBM personal computers from local retailers, upgrading them in his dorm room, and selling them not only around campus but in the local community. His revenues were $180,000—in the first month alone! Unfortunately, he dropped out of college, convinced he could make a living doing something he loved. Today he has to live with the curse of being a college dropout and the shame of being worth only $13 billion. In 2006, Dell Inc. was recognized by *Fortune* magazine as one of America's top twenty-five most admired companies.

Michael Dell found an idea that fit his skills, created his own work doing something he loved, and gave people something they wanted. Too often, when selecting a product or service to sell, people put the cart before the horse. They look for trends or hot opportunities, frequently overlooking their own unique talents,

POT-SHOTS
Brilliant Thoughts in 17 Words or Less

©ASHLEIGH BRILLIANT 2003.   POT- SHOTS NO.9553.

PEOPLE WHO ARE MORE INTERESTED IN THE WORK THAN IN THE MONEY USUALLY MAKE MORE MONEY.

Ashleigh Brilliant.com

---

abilities, and interests. I tell clients repeatedly that 85 percent of the process of having confidence about proper direction is to look inward first. Identify your strongest areas of competence, your personality traits, and your passions. The remaining 15 percent is then the application of those into meaningful work. I would rather help someone expand on a natural interest in dandelions than force her to be successful in the latest technology just because it's seen as a growth trend.

In his book *The Millionaire Mind,* Thomas Stanley looked at the common characteristics of those who ended up decamillionaires in America. The common themes were not found in IQ, GPA, college major chosen, business selected, or profession developed. *The only factor the extremely successful people shared in common was that they all were doing something they loved.*

Be confident that you can find great opportunities that will also allow you to be true to yourself. Over 2 million new businesses will be started this year—will yours be one of them? The opportunities are all around you, so be on the lookout for new ideas. You may have to look with new eyes, but the possibilities have never been greater.

You may need to unclutter your life so you have the brain space to recognize new ideas. If you gather a group of thirty children when they are five years old and ask how many can sing, every hand will go up. How many can dance? Every hand goes up. How many can draw? Again, every hand goes up. If you wait thirteen years and ask the same group the same questions at age eighteen, only about half will claim any of those skills. Wait another seventeen years and ask the same group at age thirty-five, and you'll see only two or three hands raised in the entire group. What happened? Are you one of those whose dreams have been numbed by the realities of life? Can you even remember what your dreams were? Do you believe God birthed those dreams originally or were they just the foolish ideas of a naive child? Take this time in your life, wherever you are, to take a fresh look at those dreams that have been dormant and to reaffirm those unique talents that have just become rusty and neglected.

Here are some methods to help you rebirth your genius.

Revolutionary Insight

The Upside-Down Christmas Tree

Well here's a novel new Christmas tradition—the Upside-Down Christmas Tree.[1] And can you guess why anyone would want an upside-down tree? With the growing greed and expectation of stuff, this tree allows more room for presents. Why settle for the traditional tree, with the limited amount of space around the bottom, when you can have just the tip of the tree interfering with piles of plastic toys and gadgets?

Standing at seven feet tall and prelit with over eight hundred commercial-grade lights, this technological marvel can be yours for the low price of $599.95. According to Hammacher Schlemmer's website: "The inverted shape makes it easier to see ornaments, which hang away from the dense needles" while "allowing more room for the accumulation of presents underneath." Only in America!

Sew Up Your Buttonholes?

I once read a story in William Danforth's classic little book *I Dare You!* about a professor who hit upon a great discovery while buttoning up his vest—or rather, he hit upon the discovery because his vest *wouldn't* button up.[2] It turns out his little daughter had sewn up some of the buttonholes by mistake, and as his fingers were going along in the usual motions of buttoning a button, something happened. A button wouldn't button.

The fingers fumbled helplessly for a moment, then sent out a call for help. The professor's mind woke up. His eyes looked down, and a new idea was born, or rather a new understanding of an old idea. What the professor had discovered was that fingers can remember. You know how repetitive certain tasks—such as riding a bicycle, using a keyboard, or even driving home from the office—can become, so much so that our brains essentially go on autopilot.

With this new knowledge in place, the professor began playing pranks on his classes, testing his thesis. He soon found that the results were always the same. As long as they could keep on doing the things they had always done, his students' minds wouldn't work at optimum capacity. It was only when he figuratively sewed up their buttonholes by stealing their notebooks, locking the doors, or upsetting their routine that any creative thinking was done.

So he came to the great, and now generally accepted, conclusion that the human mind is "an emergency organ"—that it relegates whatever it can to automatic functions for as long as it can. It is only when something upsets the old order of things that the mind really starts working.

So my advice is this: Sew up some buttonholes in your life. Drive a different route home from work. Read a book you would not normally read. Take time to help a stranded motorist. Volunteer for a community project. Take a walk with a child and really watch how she responds to things you take for granted. Sit quietly for twenty minutes one morning—not reading or praying—but just listening for and expecting new spiritual insight. And welcome the unexpected closed buttonholes this week. You may be surprised at what happens when you allow your brain to turn on. Who knows what creative ideas or solutions you may discover?

Focus on Your Weaknesses—and Get Strong Weaknesses

In the sixth grade, a teacher told my friend Phil that the "secret to life is to focus on your weaknesses." So for the next thirty years he worked on those areas where he was weakest. He struggled with accounting, with organization, and with ordering and inventory control. He ultimately developed some pretty strong . . . weaknesses. Then he discovered the power of focusing on your strengths. He surrounded himself with people who were more competent in all the areas where he was weak. He allowed them to do what they did well while he did the same.

Today he is a multimillionaire. He has no office because he has competent people handling all his business functions from their own offices. He excels at creating the vision while encouraging these people to carry out the daily tasks.

How sad that we often diminish our best gifts by struggling valiantly to develop in someone else's area of ability. It is better to focus on your unique skills and do them with excellence than to end up performing at a mediocre level in several areas. Use this rule of thumb for organizing your work strategy:

Work where you are the strongest 80 percent of the time.
Work where you are learning 15 percent of the time.
Work where you are weak 5 percent of the time.[3]

I frequently tell people that there are twenty to twenty-five components of my business. I probably do a pretty good job at two or three of those. As for the rest, I allow people who are

Revolutionary Insight

Don't Be a Goose . . .

In a classic fable, a grazing goose found herself annoyed by a horse who was eating nearby. In hissing accents, the goose addressed the horse: "I am certainly a more noble and perfect creature than you, for the whole range and extent of your abilities is confined to one element. I can walk upon the ground as you do; I have besides, wings, with which I can raise myself in the air; and when I please, I can sport on ponds and lakes, and refresh myself in the cool waters. I enjoy the different powers of a bird, a fish, and a horse."

The horse, with seasoned wisdom, replied: "It is true you inhabit three elements, but you make no very distinguishing figure in any one of them. You fly indeed; but your flight is so heavy and clumsy, that you have no right to put yourself on a level with the lark or the swallow. You can swim on the surface of the waters, but you cannot live in them as fishes do; you cannot find your food in that element, nor glide smoothly along the bottom of the waves. And when you walk, or rather waddle, upon the ground, with your broad feet and your long neck stretched out, hissing at everyone who passes by, you bring upon yourself the derision of all beholders. I confess that I am only formed to move upon the ground; but how graceful is my make! How great my strength! How astonishing my speed! I had much rather be confined to one element, and be admired in that, than be a goose in all!"

Wow! The goose sounds like some people I know. They try to be good at marketing, computers, financial planning, supervising, administration, and selling—rather than focusing on one or two areas of excellence. *Find the area where you run like the wind, with few competitors. Then you'll rise from mediocrity and experience uncommon success.*[4]

much more competent than I am to perform with excellence in their areas. I am a novice when it comes to Internet details, yet we use cutting-edge technology to drive the success of our e-commerce. I hate the details of accounting and financial management, so I've engaged a CPA to handle those areas efficiently and create simple reports I can understand. What are two or three areas in which you excel? How could you change your current circumstances to focus on those areas?

Looking for New Ideas

How many times have you had an idea that you forgot about, only to see it in reality three years later? It appears that someone else had the same idea but acted on it. Start tracking your ideas. You may want to keep a journal, a folder on your computer, or audio notes on a handy recorder. If you *expect* to have three or four ideas every week, you'll be amazed to see them accumulate quickly. You'll begin to see recurring themes that will allow you to put action plans in place to bring them to life. Even if you've not had your million-dollar idea yet, here are some ways to help you see new ideas and opportunities.

Attend Seminars

Go to any event that will give you a new way to look at ideas. Recognize that success principles are universal and transferable. For example, I have gotten many great ideas for marketing and building a business from real estate seminars, although I have no interest in real estate investing or selling. Go to the free business seminars. Often, they will offer opportunities for you to buy something. That's okay—you don't have to spend any money! Just take the good information, even if you don't want that particular business idea. Watch your Sunday paper for free workshops and seminars in your area.

Listen to Training CDs

If there is one way to transform your success quickly, I believe it is in listening to audio programs. Years ago, I calculated the following: The person who drives a car 25,000 miles a year, at an average speed of forty-six miles per hour, will spend approximately the same amount of time in that car as a college student spends in the classroom in a year of study. If you're calculating, that's about 543 hours. Some of you spend that much time just in a daily commute. A little more than two hours each day, five days a week, fifty weeks a year will translate into the same amount of time. Which brings me to the question, What do you do with that time? Do you just *spend* it listening to meaningless (or even negative) music (chewing gum for the mind), or do you *invest* it in a way that can take you to a higher level of success? I have seen clients learn new languages, improve their ability to sell, and start new businesses based on this simple process of capturing the time they were already spending in their cars. Most public libraries have audio sets you can borrow at no cost, like books. Nightingale-Conant is the largest provider of motivational and learning tape sets. Contact them at http://www.nightingale .com and request a free catalog.

Read Magazines

If you are serious about looking at new options, you must be reading current magazines to help expand your thinking. Too often people simply hear about one idea and decide they will try to duplicate someone else's success. The process of finding the right idea for you is to look at one hundred ideas before deciding. This is like buying a house or a car; you don't just go out and take the first one you see. Look at many and you will learn how to recognize the best one for you. Pick up magazines like *Entrepreneur, Business Start-Ups, Income Opportunities, Working from Home Inc., Fast Company, Success, Fortune, BusinessWeek,* or *Money.*

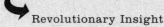

Revolutionary Insight

This Will Cost You . . .

People often ask me how I find time to read as much as I do. (I read at least one new book a week.) The answer is that I'm afraid not to. When I crashed in business, in 1988, I made a commitment to spend two hours a day reading, listening, praying, and meditating on positive, encouraging material. The results were so obvious that now I find that when I want to jump forward in a new venture or area of success, I *increase* that time commitment.

Jim Rohn, perhaps the world's leading motivator and speaker, says you can judge a person's bank account by the size of his or her library. The marketing guru Dan Kennedy says he's observed that people with tiny bank accounts tend to have no libraries, but they usually have big TVs.

A Stanford University study has indicated that if you read thirty to sixty minutes each day in your field of interest, in four to five years you will be a national authority.

All leaders are readers. Studies show that those who are readers are more positive, optimistic, and excited. Those who are not readers are more negative, pessimistic, and doubtful about their future.

Two books read by virtually all successful people are *Think and Grow Rich* by Napoleon Hill and *How to Win Friends and Influence People* by Dale Carnegie.

I know of no quicker and surer way to jump to a higher level of success in your career, relationships, or bank account than to read. As Mr. Rohn says, "It isn't what the book costs; it's what it will cost you if you don't read it."

The man who never reads will never be read; he who never quotes will never be quoted. He who will not use the thoughts of other men's brains proves he has no brain of his own.

—Charles H. Spurgeon

Read Books

There are wonderful books out there to encourage you and stretch your thinking, and they are not only the latest books to hit the bestseller lists. Success is not only universal, it is also timeless. Principles for success can be found in many of the old classics. In addition, take advantage of the current flood of new material. Send me an e-mail at reading@48Days.com, and you'll instantly get my current recommendations.

Get Rid of Your TV

This may sound rash, but if you are spending two to three hours a day in front of the TV, it is highly unlikely that you will experience unusual success. Successful people simply have identified things that create a greater return than the mindless drivel presented on the great percentage of TV programs. They are also very protective of what goes into their minds, recognizing that our minds are like computers—garbage in, garbage out. If you are going to watch TV, make it a positive experience. Subscribe to The Success Training Network and for pennies a day bring the brightest minds in the world into your living room.

Spend Thirty Minutes a Day Reflecting and Learning

In the bestselling tape series of all time, *The Psychology of Winning*, Denis Waitley guarantees that if a salesperson will spend just thirty minutes a day listening, learning, and growing, he or she will double results in six months. Even if the growth is only 15 percent in a year, output will still double in four years. That's the power of compounding your growth.

Embrace Failure

This may sound too radical. But those who cannot tolerate failure will always take the safe route. Starting on your own is not like gambling—with a careful plan you dramatically reduce any risk. Anything outside the ordinary does have a certain degree of risk. And with risk, there is always the possibility of failure. However, as Rhett Butler says in the movie *Scarlett*, "Whenever there is the possibility of failure there is also the possibility of winning." Robert Schuller compares this process to a high jumper approaching the bar. As long as he clears the bar every time, we don't know how good the jumper is. It's only when he trips the bar (failure) that we have a true measure of how good he is. Rick Pitino, the great basketball coach at the University of Louisville, says, "Failure is the fertilizer of success."

There are many additional ways to expand your list of ideas.

I had a recent conversation with Noe Torres, my landscape and yard maintenance manager. His dad lives in a Mexican city of about fifty thousand residents. Like many people who have relatives here, his dad has been waiting each week for the check from his sons who live and work in the United States.

Noe and his brother are true entrepreneurs—and they began to look for opportunities to help their dad be more self-sufficient. He has always had a dream of operating a little ice cream shop in Mexico. So Noe purchased a couple of small freezers at Home Depot here in the States for $150 each and took them down to his dad. He built a forty-by-eighty-foot warehouse and purchased a machine that makes 2,500 ice pops in eight hours. They made ice cream and stocked those little freezers with ice cream goodies. They then offered to place them in mom-and-pop stores around the city. No money required—they simply come back the next week, restock the freezers, and split the proceeds from anything that has sold.

At this point they have twenty-three freezers in place. The store owners love it, and Noe's dad is living out his dream. He is also employing about ten grandchildren, who are now making their own money for school clothes and supplies by helping to stock and deliver the freezers. The average daily income in this city is $10 to $15. Mr. Torres is currently making about $150 a day, and his sons are projecting that will grow to $500 a day within another six months. A whole family has been removed from the "welfare" expectations, and a new generation is learning the principles of working and managing money with an opportunity right in their own backyard.

Yes, the grass frequently appears greener on the other side of the fence. But in reality the grass is greenest where it gets watered most. Is there an idea right in your backyard that could change your family's financial condition?

Chatting with a friend, attending a concert, going to a museum, the movies, or a sports event, even just stopping at the dry cleaners on a Saturday morning may be all you need to do to release your million-dollar idea.

Revolutionary Insight

"It's Hard to Sing the Blues When You're Doing So Well"

My wife, Joanne, and I have had the pleasure of hearing Dottie Rambo, the prolific gospel songwriter with over twenty-five hundred published songs to her credit. After listening to one of her recent compilations, I was attracted to this title: "It's Hard to Sing the Blues When You're Doing So Well." It reminded me that some people just seem to take pride in doing poorly so they can keep singing the blues. You know the kind—the ones you hate to ask "How are you doing?" because you're afraid they'll tell you. Some of these people wouldn't have anything to talk about if they were not complaining, accusing, blaming, and finger-pointing. Yes, and I do see people who sabotage their own success—apparently convinced that failure is easier to handle.

Personally, I enjoy moving beyond singing the blues.

Give the best you have, and it will never be enough. Give your best anyway.

—Mother Teresa

Look Inward

The continuing process of looking inward is a critical part of iden-tifying a work model that fits you. As you get to know yourself better, you will also learn how to eliminate ideas that do not fit you—even if the ideas or opportunities are hot trends. Subway is the hottest selling franchise but would not be a fit for you unless you enjoy managing entry-level employees and are free to com-mit evening and weekend hours to your work. Many network marketing ideas offer the potential of explosive income but fit only a few select people who are skilled at recruiting and moti-vating others. Build your own filter for sorting and evaluating the hundreds of ideas that you should explore. By this process you will accurately narrow the options. Remember that 85 percent of having the confidence of proper direction comes from looking in-ward; only 15 percent is creating the appropriate application. Don't get the cart before the horse!

POT-SHOTS
Brilliant Thoughts in 17 Words or Less

©ASHLEIGH BRILLIANT 1993. SANTA BARBARA.   POT-SHOTS NO. 6352.

WHY IS PLEASURE
SO OFTEN CONSIDERED
A WASTE OF TIME,

WHILE SUFFERING IS CONSIDERED
MEANINGFUL
AND WORTHWHILE?

Ashleigh
Brilliant

Looking Inward Questions

- Do you like people, ideas, or things?
- Are you creative and expressive or logical and analytical?
- Are you neat and orderly or carefree and unorganized?
- Are you a social butterfly or a recluse?
- Do you easily influence people or cringe at the thought of disciplining an employee?
- What are five things you enjoy doing in your free time?
- List any technical or unique skills you possess.
- What personal qualities account for the greatest success in your life so far?
- List five things other people say you do well.
- What are your background, education, and experience?
- What do you want to be part of your workday? Time freedom, opportunity to help others, more money, chance to develop a hobby, et cetera?

My Possibilities . . .

Now list twenty business ideas that would allow you to incorporate the items just listed. Stretch your thinking. Don't stop until you reach twenty. (This is a process I have used with high achievers for years. Often they come in with one great idea, but I require that they come up with nineteen more before we create a plan of action. It's uncanny how, in that process, a new option often rises to the top as the best choice.)

The future is not some place we are going, but one we create. The paths are not found, but made, and the activity of making them changes both the maker and the destination.

—John Schaar

Some Additional Possibilities

- *Improving* an existing product or service is the surest and quickest way to success.
- Brand-new products or services are usually very *risky*.
- Don't look for *get rich quick* schemes. If it sounds too good to be true, it probably is.
- Look at the *long-term perspective*.
- *Decide to be excellent* at whatever you do. This provides more leverage than any other factor.

More on Looking for New Ideas

- Go to trade shows.

If you're looking for an idea, just start looking at what is being done in that area. Think about how you can expand or improve what is already out there. Look for opportunities to distribute products, or affinity groups who will purchase products you create. The hottest affinity group in the world is Harley-Davidson riders—that means they'll buy nearly anything with the Harley-Davidson logo on it. And they are just one example of many like-minded groups you can target. Pam Stahl has always enjoyed quilting—and she's not the only one. At her website, http://www.RealWomenQuilt.com, Pam connects the quilting community and provides them with great books, fabrics, gifts, and other fun quilting stuff. How'd she get started? She went to a quilting conference and just by walking around talking to people

Revolutionary Insight

"Invent" the Ordinary

Stanley Mason died in December 2005 at the age of eighty-four. In his last fifty years, he introduced over one hundred inventions and acquired fifty-five patents, including the squeezable ketchup bottle, granola bars, heated pizza boxes, heatproof plastic microwave cookware, dental floss dispensers, the underwire bra, and "instant" splints and casts for broken limbs.

Mason created his first invention at the age of seven; it was a clothes-pin fishing lure that he sold to his friends. In 1949, Mason had his first major breakthrough: changing his baby boy's diapers inspired him to invent, and later patent, the world's first disposable, pin-free diapers, contoured to fit a baby's bottom.

He spent most of his time in worthwhile charitable activities but had a simple business and income goal: He would invent at least one product a year that would make him a million dollars, thus freeing up his time for worthy causes.

In his late twenties, while working for the American Can Company, Mason was called in to see the CEO and assumed he was getting a raise. "I understand you are working on a disposable diaper," Mason quoted the chairman as saying. "Don't you know that no one will ever use a disposable diaper? We got along without you before you came, and we'll get along after you leave. Good-bye."

"You should always be fired in America," Mason told the *Fairfield County Business Journal* in 1998. "That is how you get ahead."

Stanley Mason invented simple things for practical daily use. His career stands as proof that an aspiring inventor needs neither abstract theory nor high technology to become a major success. There are still plenty of opportunities for great ideas.

was able to launch her newsletter with sixteen hundred subscribers.

• Ask your friends. They'll often have great ideas. Of course, keep in mind that everyone has ideas, but you are the person who is going to put a plan together. Also keep in mind that some of your friends may not be supportive of your new ideas.

Some time ago I put this quotation by Jim Rohn in my weekly newsletter: "You are the average of the five people you spend the most time with." I think I got more comments on that than any quotation I've ever used. Now here's another interesting fact. Do you know that most people earn within 20 percent of the average income of their closest friends? Take your ten closest friends, add their incomes together, divide by ten, and you have a measurement plus or minus 20 percent of what your income is likely to be.

• Check products being sold in foreign countries.

Even in our global economy, it's estimated that 95 percent of products are never sold outside the country where they're produced. Years ago a gentleman saw a wheelbarrow advertised in a magazine. It was fiberglass and plastic, superior to what was then available in the United States. He asked to be the U.S. distributor. He took one sample wheelbarrow to a home and garden show and received over fifty thousand orders. He did not invent it, did not patent it—he simply asked to be a distributor for an existing product. With only a $5 profit margin, that's $250,000 profit!

• Pay attention to passing fads and trendy ideas.

People have made fortunes with the Pet Rock, hula hoop, politically related T-shirts and bumper stickers, sports theme items, and other fads that present a short window of opportunity. Pet products are extremely popular right now—and millionaires are currently being made thanks to songs to make your dog happy (http://www.petcds.com/ask_animals.htm), ball caps and bandannas (http://www.schaferkennel.com), seat belts (http://www.neopaws.com/index2.html), toys (http://www.sushipups.com),

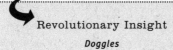

Revolutionary Insight

Doggles

The inventors of Doggles—sunglasses designed especially for dogs—say they came up with their business brain wave after noticing their dog was squinting in the sunlight. Ken and Roni di Lullo of Midnight Creations tried their own glasses on their dog's face . . . but nothing stayed on or worked well. After experimenting with sports goggles, the innovative husband-and-wife team developed a special pair to fit their dog perfectly. Other dog owners approached the couple when they were out walking, and a business was born. After a CNN story featured Doggles, sales quadrupled overnight, and these days the di Lullos have a $1 million business. (See http://www.doggles.com.)

This is the normal process of innovation. A real person recognizes a real need and provides a solution. The most successful ideas often involve not a complicated invention process but just a simple modification of an existing product.

and health insurance. Women never tire of fancy soaps, lotions, organic oils, and perfumes as they look for beauty and sensory experiences. Health and fitness ideas never seem to fade away. Watch the news for the beginnings of fads coming your way.

• As you travel, look, listen, and learn.

Orange Julius started on the West Coast. The guy who recognized this creamy orange drink as a growing phenomenon brought it back to the Midwest and made millions. One time while we were on a family vacation, a homeless man approached us selling a paper that we later found distributed free on the street corners. I laughed when I discovered this a block or two down the street; however, that paper got me thinking about producing a similar publication in our city. When you go on a cruise, get off in those port cities, walk around, and talk to the locals. Not only will you find the best places to eat, but you may pick up an idea that could be duplicated, improved upon, or just imported.

• Make sure you find something you believe in, something you would buy yourself and use yourself, and would sell to your best friend.

• Share your ideas. Don't be secretive. Get input from everyone you know. Ideas are a dime a dozen. But the person who puts a plan of action together is the only one who will benefit. Your friends will likely be too busy to help you—or to steal your idea—but you can get their opinions and input.

• Network marketing, or multilevel marketing (MLM), is one business format where you can learn vital business skills at very little cost and risk.

Selling, organizing, making presentations, accounting, team building, negotiating, and communicating can all be learned through network marketing. But be realistic about the selling required. No matter how great the product or the company, or the friends who are inviting you to join—don't try to make yourself a kind of salesperson that you are not.

• Eighty-five percent of what you need to know about running a successful business you can learn from running a successful mail-order or eBay business. You can experiment with nearly all the necessary components of a traditional business and adjust your work model as you learn.

This is another method to explore a business with very little risk on the front end. A few years ago, a woman ran a simple two-line ad in the back of a couple of women's magazines promoting her list "101 Ways to Fix Hamburger." She collected thousands of dollars from people sending her their $2.95 for that list. She then did the same thing with "101 Ways to Fix Chicken." A client of mine once wrote a little eight-page pamphlet titled "How to Land an Airplane Safely." By running an ad in flying magazines, he collected over $12,000 in about six months. Another client created her own pattern for folding a handkerchief in the shape of an angel. She promoted that pattern and generated $1,200 to $1,500 a month for nearly a year during a difficult divorce and transition to creating her own income.

You have probably seen the late-night TV ads with Don Lapre, Brad Richdale, Carleton Sheets, Dave Del Dotto, Matthew Lesko, and hundreds of others promoting their materials to teach you how to get rich quickly and with very little work. Or the Internet blasts of Yanik Silver, Armand Morin, Alex Mandossian, Robert Allen, and others. You are promised wealth by using their latest, greatest systems for real estate investing, affiliate marketing, self-publishing, selling lists of moneymaking ideas, and more. Obviously, they are making a lot of money by selling us the information. Is it legitimate? Some of it is. Is it overpriced? Probably. But the key is that these ideas are potential income producers only if *you* create a realistic plan of action.

Having information never made anyone any money, but if you find an idea and start experimenting, you can, in fact, make a lot of money. Start by testing small and then moving up in the volume of your promotion. Don't be afraid to invest in these moneymaking promotions. Don't feel bad if they really don't teach you anything new. Just see it as part of the process of learning. Think back to how much of what you learned in high school or college really isn't that useful. It was just part of the process. See yourself as a *continuing learner*. Learn from twenty different sources. Somewhere in that process you'll find the two or three ideas that will launch your next level of success.

What I lack is to be clear in my mind what I am to do, not what I am to know. . . . The thing is to understand myself, to see what God really wished me to do. . . . To find the idea for which I can live and die.

—Søren Kierkegaard

If You're a Revolutionary, You Will

- Sew up your buttonholes now and then.
- Focus on your strengths—not your weaknesses.
- Set aside prayer and meditation time expecting problem solutions.
- Become an idea magnet.
- Look inward to create your idea filter.

11

NO MONEY—NO PROBLEM!

The Root of All Evil . . .

In 1900 there were fewer than 5,000 millionaires in the United States. Today there are nearly 9 million millionaires and 40 billionaires.[1] And 979,000 more became millionaires last year—approximately one every two minutes. Where do these new millionaires get their money? Are you capable of joining their ranks? And, more important, would you even want to be one of them?

Now, I know that's a reasonable question, because I hear so many conflicting positions on having money. Growing up in a very conservative Mennonite home, I learned that you don't talk about money and you certainly don't let anyone know you want more.

We know money is the root of all evil, right? No, of course not; this is not the Biblical principle at all. It's the *love* of money that is the root of all evil. And who do you think loves money more—those who have it, or those who want it?

I don't hear the wealthy people I know talking about money nearly as much as I do my acquaintances who are struggling; those without wealth seem to relate to everything they do in terms of how much money it will cost or generate. So who really is a slave to money, the person who is doing something he or she loves and in the process making $250,000 a year? No, it's the person who, each day, goes to a job he or she hates, *just for the money*—there's the person who has made money his or her god. There's the person who focuses on and *loves* money.

This is a difficult point for most people. A lot of us hold on to the primitive religious belief that poverty and self-sacrifice are pleasing to God. Somehow this implies that God has finished his work, has made all that he can make, and so the majority of people must stay poor because there's not enough to go around. Too many good people are ashamed of wanting much for fear they may deprive others of having their needs met. But as I see it, the reverse is true. The best way to help the poor is to reduce their numbers by not being one of them.

The desire for wealth need not be associated with greed; it can, rather, arise out of our innate capacity for growth and fulfillment. In his now classic 1910 book, *The Science of Getting Rich,* Wallace Wattles said, "That which makes you want more money is the same as that which makes the plant grow; it is life seeking fuller expression." What God requires is that we use our talents wisely—and what you will see in return is a release of peace, a sense of accomplishment, and *money.*

If a person gets his attitude toward money straight, it will help straighten out almost every other area in his life.

—Billy Graham

If you try to convince yourself that you don't want money, that you just want to serve others, that you want to devote your life to humanitarian efforts, you will subtly sabotage your efforts. Even if you want to start a nonprofit organization, unless you figure out quickly how to have more income than expenses, you will find you have no opportunity to do the work you have been called to do. I have seen many competent and honorable individuals say, "I'm just trusting God," or "I just want to make the world a better place," only to end up frustrated because they have no vehicle for honoring God or improving the world. Don't follow this foolish path. If you make it one of your goals to make money and a lot of it, you will find your opportunities for service will increase dramatically. Convince yourself you don't care about making money, and you will likely end up with nothing that benefits you or anyone else.

I received hundreds of responses to an article I wrote on this subject titled "The Root of All Evil." One reader wrote: "It has taken me sixty years to come to the point of agreeing with Dan. Many of those years I helped carry the load of and for others at the expense of my family because I didn't think I deserved more." Here's another of my favorites: "Dan, the thought that I have had for years is 'I just want enough money to get by.' In turn, that is all I ever had." Ah, yes, as the Bible says, "As a man thinketh in his heart, so is he."

Revolutionary Income

As we have already discussed, there are many reasons for seeking out revolutionary models of work. Money is not usually the first; most people are more motivated by time control and freedom. But almost everyone I meet agrees that the potential to increase his or her income is certainly attractive as well. This chapter will answer the question "Is it really possible to make money without being employed by a big company?" And the answer is a resounding yes. In fact, working for a company significantly reduces one's chances of ever becoming wealthy. Common sense alone should indicate the red flags. For a company to *hire* someone, that person's effort must generate three to five times his or her salary. Simple mathematics would imply that, by moving out of the employee model, a person should be able to work less and make more money immediately. A couple of years ago I helped an interior designer move from a $15-an-hour salary to a

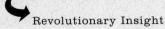

Revolutionary Insight

Millionaire by When?

Want to be a millionaire? Here's a calculator that allows you to plug in your basic information and learn how old you'll be when you hit the millionaire status. Put in some figures just to test it. Hopefully you'll be a millionaire while you're still young enough to enjoy it. (See http://swz .salary.com/millionairemaker.)

$40-an-hour income for her freelance work. Almost immediately, she moved on from that to a $100,000-plus-a-year income by doing projects rather than even positioning herself for hourly compensation.

Here is a breakdown of the millionaires in America.[2]

BUSINESS OWNERS: 74 PERCENT This category includes typical entrepreneurs, Eaglepreneurs, real estate agents, et cetera. You don't have to reinvent the wheel or patent something to be very successful. You can do freelance graphic design, bookkeeping, lawn maintenance, or product delivery and find yourself in this category immediately.

SENIOR EXECUTIVES: 10 PERCENT This group includes people like Lee Iacocca or Jack Welch, who stayed in their industries for years and worked their way up to high-paying positions. But remember, in today's work environment, longevity and seniority are not necessarily going to be rewarded. Results are what get noticed, so these senior executive positions are often awarded to someone outside the organization. One may quickly reach CEO, CFO, and other senior positions if one can prove one's ability to get the job done; however, there is little traditional security in any of these positions.

DOCTORS, LAWYERS, AND OTHER PROFESSIONALS: 10 PERCENT Some people in these professions grow wealthy, but not all of them. Many feel the pressure to present a certain standard of living and therefore live highly consumptive lifestyles, never accumulating any real wealth. Even high income for services does not guarantee wealth. It is only those professionals who live on much less than they make and put some money to work for them who go on to become wealthy.

SALESPEOPLE AND CONSULTANTS: 5 PERCENT This list can include people from any industry. Success in these fields usually has little to do with educational degrees, licensure, or certification; good salespeople are simply people who are very good at selling, and good consultants have demonstrated such a proficiency in a given area that others are willing to pay for their services. Selling and consulting are great equalizers. People with an eighth-grade education or a PhD can be at the same level within thirty days, using these skills as their wealth generator.

STOCK BROKERS, INVENTORS, ACTORS, DIRECTORS, AUTHORS, SONGWRITERS, ATHLETES, LOTTERY WINNERS: ABOUT 1 PERCENT Since this category contains the professions most frequently noticed and talked about, it may come as a shock to you that only 1 percent of millionaires belong to this category. After all, every little kid wants to be the next Tiger Woods, Alan Jackson, Michael Jordan, Penélope Cruz, Toni Morrison, or Cindy Crawford. But celebrities like these, along with members of all the other professions listed here, compose less than 1 percent of America's millionaires. Statistically, you have a much greater chance of becoming a millionaire by going out and buying a $138 lawn mower and starting a yard service today.

Remember, you don't need to reinvent the wheel to launch your own successful venture. Just do something *10 percent* better than the competition or provide *added value*. You can look at this list and decide where you have the best chances of creating your wealth. If you are an artist, actress, inventor, or the next Robin Williams, then believe that you can be in the 1 percent category. But I would guess that, for most of you, the chances for true wealth are going to be greatest by seeing yourselves in the 74 percent category. And the wonderful thing is that you can put yourself in that group today. Please recognize that even if you love writing, art, music, theater, or sports, you may seek an immediate advantage by applying those passions in the self-owned business category. Rather than waiting to be discovered, you could write an e-book and market it on the Internet. You could open a used sports equipment business or become an agent for actors or musicians; that way, you'd still experience the satisfaction of immersing yourself in your passion while reaping the security and other benefits that come from a significant income.

The best way to predict the future is to invent it.
—Alan Kay

In today's traditional workplace, *security* is an illusion. When you are working for a company, your fate is in the hands of one person—your boss (or, even worse, the shareholders and executives who see you as fixed overhead, not a person). A decision by one person, one who might not even know your name, can put you out on the street. But in your own business, if you are selling hot dogs on the street corner, every one of your customers would have to fire you before you're out of business. If you are selling products on eBay, you have 222 million potential customers from all over the world—having one who doesn't like you or your product does not put you out of business.

As General Douglas MacArthur said, "Security is the ability to produce." Your security is in knowing clearly what it is that you do well and then doing that with excellence.

Uncertainty—the sense of not knowing what lies ahead—is the only context in which we can create a future that will be different from the past. When everything is certain and predictable, there can only be a repeat of what has been before. We know that faith, by definition, means not knowing what is coming. That's why faith involves confidently taking the next step based on what God has revealed to you. Uncertainty means anything is possible. Not having things handed to you on a silver platter is actually an advantage.

Henry David Thoreau said: "I see young men, my townsmen, whose misfortune it is to have inherited farms, houses, barns, cattle, and farming tools; for these are more easily acquired than got rid of. Better if they had been born in the open pasture and suckled by a wolf, that they might have seen with clearer eyes what field they were called to labor in."[3]

Frequently I see that those who have been given advantages early in life find themselves with a strong sense of being off track in their forties or fifties. I have a friend who, while a gifted singer and performer, has never developed these or any other talents as he is too busy protecting the money he inherited from his father. A current client was given the best education money could buy, including medical school, and now, at age fifty-two, realizes he has never pursued his real calling. The search for authentic work is a very personalized and internal one and can easily be derailed by too many advantages. The best medical, dental, or law school will never provide a fulfilling career path if that path is not a match with the unique gifts of the person involved. Just as you shouldn't let a lack of money deter you from pursuing a great opportunity now, don't let money you already have keep you from moving toward your passion.

I was raised in a poor farming family in rural Ohio. Not quite Thoreau's "born in the open pasture," but almost. My dad is now ninety-five and living in a retirement center. My siblings and I will likely be called on to subsidize his stay there in the very near future. My inheritance was a strong work ethic, seeing an example of godly integrity and character, observing my parents' sixty-two year marriage, and being called a "wise son" by my dad. That's enough for me. Beyond that, it was up to me to find my path and live it out.

A wise man should have money in his head,
but not in his heart.

—Jonathan Swift

Money Won't Buy Happiness

I love moneymaking ideas. And I love to see people start businesses and go on to earn extraordinary wealth. But the eventual wealth is not the only reward. The process of *earning* money itself can be an incredibly enlightening lesson. We learn the value of a hard-earned dollar, we learn how to duplicate the process, we learn how to live full and enriched lives, and we learn how to enjoy sharing with others who have not yet had the same opportunities.

Unfortunately, people who get money without working for it often miss all those benefits. Lottery winners, lawsuit recipients, and people who inherit money often find their instant wealth to be their undoing. In 2000, the forklift operator Mack Metcalf and his wife, Virginia, won a $34 million jackpot. Years of blue-collar struggles gave way overnight to limitless leisure, pleasures, and toys. A divorce, new lovers, all-terrain vehicles, vintage cars, houses, drugs, exotic pets, and unpaid child support came quickly thereafter. Mr. Metcalf went from being a forklift operator to living a life that seemingly destroyed him. Within three years, he was dead at age forty-five of complications from chronic alcoholism. His wife died in 2005 at the age of fifty-one. Drug overdose is suspected, although that has not been confirmed.

Be very careful about wanting money that you did not earn. The process of getting wealth—not the money itself—is what has value. Money will only make you more of what you already are. Make sure you are making deposits of success in meaningful life areas—while you are accumulating money.

> The trustworthy will get a rich reward. But the person who wants to get rich quick will only get into trouble.
>
> —Proverbs 28:20 (NLT)

Sources of Money for Starting a Business

There are typically three reasons people never act on their dreams to achieve the financial independence they desire.

1. The first reason is *fear of failure.* There is nothing more crippling than fear of failure. I've seen otherwise intelligent people who are so afraid of failure they let idea after idea pass them by, only to regret their inaction. Remember the words of Paul: "For God hath not given us the spirit of fear; but of power, and of love, and of a sound mind" (2 Timothy 1:7, KJV).

2. The second reason is *lack of knowledge.* Creative, nontraditional, or innovative skills are not just things you stumble onto. You have to learn how to invest, how to deal in real estate, how to evaluate business opportunities, or perhaps how to manage employees. But these are all things that can be learned and should never prevent you from exploring new options for a better life.

3. The third reason people don't act on their dreams is a perceived *lack of money.* I stress *perceived* because money is not really what's holding them back. People *think* they don't have enough money to take the first steps toward revolutionary work, but the

problem usually comes back to fear of failure or lack of knowledge.

I get eight to ten requests per week from people wanting to
know where to find start-up money for new ventures. And, yes,
capital is difficult to find—especially for businesses that use service, information, or technology. Does that mean it's impossible to
launch a great idea without start-up capital? Absolutely not! Take
a look at this recent Census Bureau data:

- 26 percent of business start-ups didn't require any
  capital
- 34 percent needed less than $5,000
- 9 percent needed $5,000–$9,999
- 12 percent needed $10,000–$24,999
- 6 percent needed $25,000–$49,999
- 5 percent needed $50,000–$99,000
- 4 percent needed $100,000–$249,999
- 3 percent needed $250,000–$999,999
- 1 percent needed $1 million or more

No Money—No Problem!

If 69 percent of all new businesses need less than $10,000 to get
started and 70 percent of the people on the street say they would
like to start their own business, why don't they? A young couple
came to see me desperately wanting to open a coffeehouse. The
"experts" told them they needed between $180,000 and $220,000
to get off the ground. I helped them find a location, buy used
chairs and tables, create appealing menus, obtain a flashy neon
sign, and open to immediate success—all for less than $5,000! Af-
ter two successful years, they moved their little business into a $3
million downtown location with state-of-the-art sound and video
technology.

There are many such success stories I could share. Another gentleman bought an orange grove, using the existing oranges on the trees as his only down payment. Another purchased an old estate house, contracting to sell the antique furniture inside as his down payment. Several years ago I bought a house on a Saturday morning, gave the owner $3,000, took over the loan, did some cosmetic improvements, put it back on the market, and sold it for a $21,000 profit. Many of the best ideas today are not capital intensive. They don't require buildings, employees, and inventory. Fear of failure is a much larger obstacle than the lack of money.

"No money" is one of the most popular excuses given for not pursuing a creative or entrepreneurial idea. Chalk this up to all the talk in the media about start-up companies requiring ridiculous amounts of capital; many of the 1990s dot-com companies raised millions of dollars just to launch an idea. But the reality is that, with so many great ideas utilizing information, service, or technology as their core concept, it has never been easier to start a business with very little or no money. As we saw from the census data, 26 percent of all new businesses require no start-up capital. But here's a brief overview of where start-up money *does* come from, to encourage you and remove this perceived obstacle.

- **Banks.** Banks are not in the business of speculating on your idea. They are in the business of avoiding risks, so they will rarely loan you money unless they are convinced you have sufficient funds to repay the loan even if the business is a failure.
- **Small Business Administration loans.** Requirements for SBA loans are much the same as those of a bank. With an SBA loan, the government is not making a loan, it is simply guaranteeing a loan provided by your local bank. You can check out the requirements and get help with your loan application from your

nearest SBA bank or Small Business Development Center. (See http://www.sba.gov.)

- **Leasing.** Leasing equipment and office space can drastically reduce the need for start-up capital. For instance, if you are going to rent boats in the harbor, boat manufacturers will be happy to help you with the leasing arrangements.

- **Customer financing.** Many businesses—like Tupperware or Amway—are based on getting your order and a portion of the payment up front and the balance on delivery. This is the basic model that has been used by network marketing companies for years.

- **Supplier financing.** In the same way, it is very common to have a supplier or vendor provide merchandise that you display and sell before actually paying for it.

- **Franchising.** With this model, the franchise itself often supplies financing for a location and inventory while you are getting started.

- **Licensing.** If you have an agreement to sell T-shirts featuring the Chicago Bulls logo, you will be able to sell the shirts before paying the Bulls their share of the profits. Having a major licensing agreement strengthens your ability to sell merchandise and to get money from any of these other traditional sources.

- **Distributorships.** With my book distributorships, I order the merchandise, sell it, and collect the full price, then send the wholesale cost to the publishers.

- **Venture capital.** Venture capital funds fewer than 1 percent of new businesses. Fully 99 percent of all business ideas presented to venture capital companies are never funded in this way. Venture capitalists typically base their decisions on you, the individual, not just the business idea or product. They invest in the person and also want big, quick returns on their money—and ownership control.

• **"Love money."** More than 80 percent of new ventures are started with "love money," from people who know and trust you. They invest not primarily because they think you have a great idea but because they love you and believe in you.

Be very careful about rushing out to borrow money for your start-up idea. Horror stories abound about people who discovered the Biblical principle that "the borrower is slave to the lender." As soon as you bring in outside money for any portion of your business, you give up a large percentage of control. I have a close friend who started a business with a great idea. He then went out and raised $4 million to fund the early growth and marketing exposure. Six months after he raised the money, the board (made up of investors) decided to bring in a new CEO to lead the next stage of development. My friend was tossed out onto the street and allowed no further input into the company he birthed. If you want to stay in the driver's seat, "bootstrap"—by simply allowing your profits to grow the business.

Money is a terrible master but an excellent servant.

—P. T. Barnum

Many people don't follow their hearts and start their own ventures because they think lack of money is an insurmountable obstacle. But if you have

1. Energy
2. Ambition
3. Desire
4. Imagination

you will attract money.

Don't let the lack of money stop you from pursuing your dreams. Your personal passion and enthusiasm will open the right doors. Start by defining the reasons you want to start your own venture. Establish the *why*, and the *how-to* will appear.

For many of you, a traditional job may be the perfect way to pay rent and expenses while you develop a new idea. Mike was national director of sales for a worldwide telecommunications company. He kept his position while he began building his own training company. He set up his website, wrote his training modules, and started lining up clients—all while getting excellent performance reviews at work. After two years of planning, he was able to make a seamless transition into his own business and the fulfillment of his dream.

Robert is the director of eBay sales for a large company. As such, he oversees all product sales and essentially runs a business within a business. Having developed the systems, he saw the potential to increase his income exponentially by doing the same thing for other similar companies. I helped him prepare to present a novel idea to his current boss: he would continue exactly as agreed but would be compensated only by a percentage of

POT-SHOTS
Brilliant Thoughts in 17 Words or Less

©ASHLEIGH BRILLIANT 1992.   POT-SHOTS NO. 5737.

I'M GLAD THE FUTURE HASN'T COME YET, BECAUSE I DON'T THINK I COULD HANDLE IT RIGHT NOW.

Ashleigh Brilliant
SANTA BARBARA

sales, rather than with a salary. His boss was totally agreeable. With his boss's full knowledge and support, Robert took on four other companies and did the same for them. His income from his former employer has grown while he has added roughly four times that in income from new clients.

Karen was the director of human resources for a large manufacturing plant. The desire for more time freedom brought her to my office. We developed a multifaceted plan for her to teach four to five seminars per month for a national training organization. In addition, she teaches online courses for two universities. She now generates more income while working approximately one-third the time and spending more time caring for her horses.

In each of these examples, there was no decrease in income. A soft transition allowed these Revolutionaries to alleviate the concerns of paying for mortgages, their kids' tuition, club memberships, and groceries. And it is also worth noting that, in each of these examples, the key start-up ingredient was *intellectual* capital, not *financial* capital.

> We are told that talent creates its own opportunities. But it sometimes seems that intense desire creates not only its own opportunities, but its own talents.
>
> —Eric Hoffer

Show Me the Money!

Moving out of a traditional employee position requires that you take a totally new look at compensation. An employee expects to be paid for forty hours of work per week. A consultant can expect to bill for perhaps twenty to twenty-five hours. The rest of the forty hours will be consumed with making contacts, doing administrative work, et cetera, but it's unrealistic to expect to bill your clients for forty hours. Therefore, if you were making $15 an hour ($600 per week) as a bookkeeper and you are moving into freelance or consulting work, you would need to charge $30 an hour for twenty billable hours to duplicate that income. (Realistically, the expected rate for a bookkeeper is more like $40 to $60 per hour. If you were billing at $50 per hour for just twenty hours a week, your income would jump from $600 to $1,000 per week. That's a reasonable goal.) You should expect to increase your income significantly by making this move to freelance work. Don't plan on simply duplicating your old income—make sure you're paid what you're really worth.

Keep in mind you are now being paid for your expertise and results, not just your time. For many years I conducted a leadership development seminar for companies. It was a three-hour workshop for emerging leaders. My fee for that workshop was $3,500. Now, you can understand that no company is going to want to look at that as paying me $1,166 an hour. That sounds ridiculous. But they were purchasing a process and the result of many years of my experience—not just three hours of my time. Make sure you present your services in that light. Incidentally, I conducted those seminars only while I was building the residual income parts of my business. Remember, residual income means you work hard once and it unleashes a flow of income for months or even years. You get paid over and over again for the same effort.

While teaching seminars, even if I was being paid very well, I was generating only linear income. But the material presented the opportunity to move that to residual income as well. When I put those same leadership development principles into a three-ring binder with two CDs, it became a source of residual income for me.

When setting your rates, you have three clear choices:

1. HOURLY RATES. Find out what others are charging and make sure you give excellent value for the hours billed. Some compa-

nies like this arrangement; others will want to micromanage you if they are paying hourly.

2. **PROJECT FEES.** You may agree that you will be available for one year to teach fund-raising or sales skills. For that you will be paid $36,000. You would want to be paid the $3,000 in advance each month or perhaps even the first and last month in advance. Having three to four clients with this arrangement is a great way to start off in your new *No More Dreaded Mondays* work.

3. **MONTHLY RETAINER.** Working with a retainer gives you a set monthly fee, for which you agree to be available for certain identifiable goals. This is a very reasonable way to structure your work, and it allows you to have multiple clients. In *Million Dollar Consulting*, Alan Weiss describes how he consistently generates over a million dollars a year because of this kind of billing process.

Just be aware of the importance of this issue. Think it through carefully and create a very clear plan with income projections for your first full year.

If You're a Revolutionary, You Will

- Move past fear and lack of knowledge—act on your idea.
- Recognize that earning money is an honorable and godly endeavor.
- Be creative in seeing ways to start your business with very little capital.
- Be convinced that you can start with what you have.
- "Bootstrap" your way to growth.
- Keep accurate records from day one of every cost and transaction.

12

LIVING WITH PASSION, PURPOSE, AND PROFIT

There is a story of a ninety-two-year-old lady who was moving into a nursing home. As she was being wheeled down the corridor, the attendant began to describe the room. "I love it," the old woman gushed. "But you haven't even seen the room yet," the attendant reminded her. "That doesn't have anything to do with it," she replied. "Happiness is something you decide on ahead of time. Whether I like my room or not doesn't depend on how the furniture is arranged. It's how I arrange my mind." There's an important principle in that little story. Much of your success is decided in advance—or "arranged in your mind." Circumstances will never determine your amount of happiness. Circumstances only highlight who you already are.

By now, you have had many of your old ideas about work challenged. You have also been presented with principles for seeing new opportunities in the inevitable changes. The message is clear that change is going to continue. We can choose to hide and ignore it and be left behind, or we can embrace the change and look for the new and different opportunities.

We all tend to make decisions early in our lives that set us on paths that soon become familiar. Frequently, however, we realize that years have passed without us having seriously reevaluated that direction in light of where we now are. It's very healthy, no matter what stage of life you're in, to draw that proverbial line in the sand and take a fresh look at where you are, and where you are going.

A seasoned and "successful" gentleman wrote the following in a brief overview of his current situation: "Dan, the merry-go-round of my professional life has left me no farther than a few steps from where I got on and with a weak stomach."

Many times a career path starts because of *circumstances,* rather than *priorities.* Family expectations, chance occurrences, a friendly teacher, or the desire for money can lead us down a career path that's ultimately unfulfilling. It's tough to make choices at eighteen that will be meaningful at forty-five. Just recently, I saw a forty-four-year-old client who opened with the comment "Dan, I'm tired of living my life based on the decisions made by an eighteen-year-old."

The man who does things makes mistakes, but he never makes the biggest mistake of all—doing nothing.

—Benjamin Franklin

If your work life is not providing a sense of meaning, purpose, and fulfillment, draw that line in the sand. Decide what your ideal day would look like: How would you spend your time? What skills would you use? Money is ultimately never enough compensation for investing one's time and energy. There must be a sense of meaning and accomplishment. And yet a surprising thing frequently happens on the way to fulfillment and worthy contribution: rather than learning to live on beans and rice there is often the release of a financial flood. It's a myth that if you do what you love, then you'll have to be content to never make any money. I have had the pleasure of working with many people in this process of refocused and authentic direction, where ultimately the flow of money surprised them.

> *The rung of a ladder was never meant to rest upon, but only to hold a man's foot long enough to enable him to put the other somewhat higher.*
>
> —Thomas H. Huxley

Life is too short to stay on a merry-go-round, where there is obvious movement but the scenery never changes. Remember, however, simply by stepping off that merry-go-round, you'll have enough momentum to propel you straight out in some direction. Rather than allowing your direction to come at random, think about where you want to land. Then take that step, expecting that it will give you a jump start to a new level of success. Believe that a life of purpose and meaning is your best source of financial success as well. I hope you realize by now that it's easier to make money doing something you love than doing something you hate.

But I'm Making Good Time . . .

I've always been a big proponent of persistence. So was Calvin Coolidge, who said,

> Nothing in the world can take the place of Persistence. Talent will not; nothing is more common than unsuccessful men with talent. Genius will not; unrewarded genius is almost a proverb. Education will not; the world is full of educated derelicts. Persistence and determination alone are omnipotent. The slogan "Press On" has solved and always will solve the problems of the human race.

And yet I often see people who are persistent, determined, and . . . off track. If you are losing money on each watermelon

POT-SHOTS
Brilliant Thoughts in 17 Words or Less

© ASHLEIGH BRILLIANT 2003 · POT-SHOTS NO. 5048.

I'M ON
THE BRINK
OF
HAPPINESS ~

WILL
YOU
GIVE
ME
A PUSH?

you sell, don't buy a bigger truck in your determination to sell more. Stop what you are doing and change direction. If you are an average tennis player, don't just persist; take some lessons from a pro to learn how to be better. If you want a better marriage, ask to be mentored by someone in a great marriage. If you are miserable in your job, persistence may just get you more of what you are already experiencing. In some situations, you can work and work and nothing ever changes. It doesn't get any better; it doesn't get a lot worse. It just is what it is.

Yes, I know, we've all heard the old adage "Winners never quit, and quitters never win." Do you realize that some old adages just aren't true? If you discover you're drinking not Gatorade but antifreeze, is it admirable to persist? And yet we have lurking in the backs of our minds that quitting a job, or a business, is somehow a moral failure. We hear Vince Lombardi barking in our ears—if you were just a stronger or better person, you wouldn't quit. Winning means never quitting . . . or does it?

I want you to understand that sometimes quitting is your best strategy for moving *up*—not *down*. The easiest response under

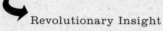

Revolutionary Insight

Take a Chance!

I am continually struck by the irony of seeing people desperately hanging on to jobs they hate. What is it that would cause a person to cling to something that is depressing and unfulfilling? What is it that causes a businessperson to continue to pour money into a losing idea?

I'm convinced that the primary factor that holds so many people back is their inability to *see* anything better than their current situation. As long as you focus on the nasty details of where you are, you are likely just to stay there and complain. Only when you get clear on what you can move *to* will you find the energy and plan to leave.

One of the most beautiful songs ever sung is Bette Midler's "The Rose," which includes this verse:

It's the heart afraid of breaking that never learns to dance.
It's the dream afraid of waking that never takes a chance.

If you feel trapped in a negative situation, start seeing what you could move *to*. And take a minute to sit back and listen to the words of this song. Turn your speakers up and bask in a few moments of beautiful music to remind you to *take a chance* for a better future. (See http://www.tahoeepiscopal.com/doc/therose2.html.)

pressure is to just continue what's not working. It takes real courage to quit—and redirect for a higher level of success. As I see people make dramatic steps forward in their personal and financial success, I often recognize their success has a lot to do with their ability to know what to *stop* doing. Typically, knowing what to stop doing is a more critical component of success than adding new activities to our busy schedules. If the road you're on is a dead end, persistence is not a helpful attribute.

Being persistent is a tactic but not a strategy. Make sure you have a strategy for each area of your life where you want to see

LIVING WITH PASSION, PURPOSE, AND PROFIT

excellence. Imagine you are driving in a Ferrari at 80 miles an hour headed straight toward Los Angeles. But you really want to go to Nashville. Accelerating to 120 miles an hour may give you the sense that you are making progress—but only temporarily. What you really need to do is change direction.

Be careful of being persistent while headed in the wrong direction. Develop strategies to find the right direction for your life.

Are You a Genius?

In 1904, Havelock Ellis noted that most geniuses were fathered by men older than thirty, had mothers younger than twenty-five, and usually were sickly children. Other researchers have reported that many were celibate (Descartes), lacking a father in the home (Dickens), or grew up without a mother (Darwin). The bottom line is that the research and data are not at all consistent. There is also no correlation between genius and intelligence. Genius seems to have little to do with getting a perfect score on your SAT, mastering quantum physics at age seven, or even being especially smart.

Genius seems to be more about the ability to see solutions that others don't. The mark of genius is a willingness to explore all the alternatives, not just the most likely solution. Asked to describe the difference between himself and an average person, Albert Einstein explained that the average person, when faced with the problem of finding a needle in a haystack, would stop when he or she found a needle. Einstein, by contrast, would tear through the entire haystack looking for all possible needles.

If you always live with those who are lame, you will yourself learn to limp.

—Latin proverb

As I've mentioned repeatedly, approaching the usual in an unusual way can often lead to new solutions. Sometimes, just purposely taking a contrarian position can offer us perspective by incongruity. In Chapter 4, I mentioned the term *Janusian thinking*—that ability to see things from two totally opposite viewpoints is often the beginning of genius thinking. Niels Bohr, a noted physicist, argued that if you hold opposites together in your mind, you will suspend your normal thinking process and allow an intelligence beyond rational thought to create new solutions. That sounds like a great place to allow the intelligence of God to find its way into our thinking. Our society tells us to stay inside the lines, but the real world and mature spiritual insight give us a blank sheet of paper and infinite creativity.

Now, what about that job search? Are you going to look at the newspaper classifieds like the thousands of others seeking work, or are you going to do something different? I once had a client who sent out his introduction letters, each wrapped around an ear of corn, along with his message: "Aw, *shucks*, I'm sure you think this is *corny*, but just give me your *ear* for a minute." Corny? Sure. But he got immediate responses, which translated into tons of opportunities.

While we're dealing with these familiar concepts of persistence, genius, and intelligence, let's examine one more. I grew up hearing all about the power of a positive mental attitude. I've read Earl Nightingale, Napoleon Hill, Zig Ziglar, Robert Schuller, and many others who all boil their teachings down to the same basic principle: What we think about, we become. The recent movie and book *The Secret*, while calling this principle the Law of Attraction, once again confirm the importance of our thoughts leading our reality.

What are you thinking? That you'll be successful? Or that you'll accept defeat? Do you believe you have some unique and clearly defined areas of competence, or do you think you're nothing special? I often tell people we end up pretty much where we expect to be. Here's a great example.

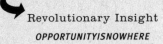

Revolutionary Insight

OPPORTUNITYISNOWHERE

I hate to be the bearer of bad news, but as I look around I see that "opportunity is nowhere." Companies are closing, people are being laid off, jobs are being outsourced, immigrants are taking all the good jobs, the economy is bad, the terrorists are taking over the world, and the sky is falling.

But wait. Maybe I misread that opening line. In looking at it again, I see that "opportunity is *now here!*" Ah yes, companies are desperately looking for good people, any job that embraces compassion and caring can't be outsourced, starting your own business has never been easier, venture capitalists are looking for good ideas for their money, many jobs now allow us to be productive into our seventies and eighties, we are still the greatest country in the world, opportunities for social entrepreneurship are exploding, and the possibilities for actually doing work you love have never been greater.

Do you know how fine that line is between seeing "no where" and "now here"?

Do you think the world is getting better, or are you convinced humanity will obliterate itself in your lifetime? Do you expect a little extra bonus in your check each week, or are you anticipating getting your walking papers? Do you think people are basically good or evil? Do you avoid setting goals so you won't be disappointed?

Do you see opportunities everywhere, or do you see that opportunity is "nowhere"? It's basically a choice. We ultimately end up pretty much where our expectations lead us. What you have in your heart and mind becomes your experience.

When Imaculee Ilibagiza came to the United States from Rwanda, she decided she wanted to work at the United Nations in Manhattan. She went to the UN website, printed out the directory that listed employees' names and titles, and then added her own name to the list. She even gave herself an imaginary telephone extension. Then she tacked the directory onto her wall where she was forced to look at it every day. Now here's the important part: She didn't *just* visualize or dream or think positively. She followed up her visualization with clear and focused action.

She filled out an application, submitted a résumé, and made persistent phone calls, trying to stay in the running with the more than a thousand other people who had applied for the same position. But she kept looking at her directory, believing the job was hers, and prayed every day until the phone rang. Sure enough, she was put on the short list of top candidates and was offered the job after her first interview.

Is this some gimmicky positive thinking? Is it tricking your mind into imagining things that aren't real? Or is it simply tapping into the power that God makes readily available to us? What do you think? Be careful about rejecting God's power for daily details as some worldly mind game. Don't overlook any of the assets available to you for fully completing God's plan for your life.

Can you see yourself moving up in your company, negotiating a more flexible schedule, or having your own successful business? And if you can, what steps of action are you going to take *next*?

People often use the following verse as an excuse for doing nothing: "But they that wait upon the LORD shall renew their strength; they shall mount up with wings as eagles; they shall run, and not be weary; and they shall walk, and not faint" (Isaiah 40:31). They focus on the word *wait* and claim they're just waiting on God. I find people who can't decide on a house to buy—and without researching real estate, they are just waiting. I've heard fathers whose children are going hungry claim they are waiting on the Lord to tell them to get a job. I talked with a forty-three-year-old man who is overweight and stressed, and has a wife who is angry because he has a two-hour commute to work. But he's waiting on the Lord to tell him to find a different job. What else does the Lord have to do to get his attention?

Do you realize that the word *wait* in Isaiah 40:31 is the same root from which we get our word *waiter*? What does it mean to be a waiter? It means you are busy doing what needs to be done—serving, checking on the needs of customers, helping, and directing. Not exactly a do-nothing stance. James added this guidance on the need for action: "As the body without the spirit is dead, so faith without deeds is dead" (James 2:26, NIV).

How Will You Create Success?

Success does not sneak into our lives in just one area. Finding fulfillment in your work will create a sense of peace and accomplishment that will spill over into other areas as well. Define what *success* means for you in all of these areas:

- Social
- Financial
- Personal development
- Spiritual
- Physical
- Family
- Career

As you clarify what success would look like for you in each of these areas, you will be able also to identify how you can make deposits in all areas simultaneously. These areas of our lives do not operate independently; they work together. Being sharp physically increases mental alertness and creativity. Those characteristics increase confidence, boldness, and enthusiasm. Confidence enhances personal relationships and spiritual vitality. Enthusiasm allows you to see opportunities that others miss. Seeing opportunities opens the door for unique applications that lead to unusual financial success.

Revolutionaries seek excellence in each of these areas and find that each can be a source of peace, fulfillment, and accomplishment. The result will lead to extraordinary success. Having fulfillment in all these areas creates a buffer if temporary difficulty or frustration occurs in one area. Trying to achieve all meaning and worth from any one area not only is a misguided goal but also puts you in a dangerous position. Furthermore, with this as a model, your job or career may change without affecting the overall direction or sense of success in your life.

Fulfilling work is simply one tool for a successful life. But it absorbs too much of our time to be ignored as a critical component of a purposeful life. Revolutionaries will set themselves apart for accomplishment, peace, and satisfaction so that they will not be in that group, who, in the words of Oliver Wendell Holmes, Jr., "like the masses, go to their graves with their music still in them."

People Do Ask, Can I Really Change My Life?

As I mentioned in the first chapter, I absolutely do believe you can change your life in a short time—*if you create a plan of action.* Obviously, if you just continue doing what you've been doing, you will continue to get exactly the same results.

The concept of a 48-Days timeline (http://www.48Days.com), with which you will be familiar if you read my previous book, grew out of the frustration I saw in people who had gotten a glimpse of what a better life could be and yet got trapped in their own version of the movie *Groundhog Day*—where they simply repeated yesterday over and over again. There has to be a timeline for taking definitive action.

48 Days is enough time to identify clearly

* Where am I?
* How can I gather the advice and opinion of others I respect?
* What are my alternatives for moving toward the life I want?
* What is the best plan of action?
* What will I do immediately to start this plan of action?

Ask yourself these questions:

1. What action can I take in the next *48 hours* to put myself on the path for what I want to accomplish?
2. What idea have I gotten while on the beach or mowing my yard that could be worth more than a lifetime of hard work?
3. What seeds did I plant in my mind five years ago that brought me to where I am today?

After considering all the options we've covered here, you are ready to create your own 48-Day plan! You can do this. You can achieve the success you are seeking. Take inventory, focus, create a plan, and *act*. You can find a free copy of the 48-Days schedule at http://www.48days.com/48dayschedule.php.

Excuses for Not Moving Forward

- "Dan, you don't know my situation. I could never do that."
- "I'm trapped where I am. I have no choices. Circumstances control me." Lack of opportunity is often nothing more than lack of purpose or direction.
- "I'll wait till all the lights are green."
- ". . . till the kids are grown."
- ". . . till I get my college degree."
- ". . . till I get some money saved up."
- "My friends and relatives will not support me."
- "I don't deserve anything better than what I have."

Solutions for Moving Forward

- Recognize that in today's work environment we have a lot of choices. Sometimes the best option involves only a subtle change from what you have been doing.
- Focus on results rather than on time, and you will open up all kinds of new opportunities.

- See that you don't have to change who you are, even if you want to do something on your own or start your own business. In the same way that we integrate skills and abilities, personality traits, and values, dreams, and passions in a traditional job, we integrate those characteristics in a creative or nontraditional choice.
- When change occurs—which it will—look for trends and new opportunities.
- Apply your purpose in meaningful, fulfilling work.
- Be excited about entering the most significant season of your life.

> The secret of success in life is for a man to be ready for his opportunity when it comes.
>
> —Benjamin Disraeli

I believe we can all find, or create, meaningful work. Yes, it's much more than just earning a paycheck. Most of us express a desire to make the world a better place. Each of us is equipped with unique skills to accomplish that. We don't all need to find positions with nonprofits or church organizations; rather, finding work that is an authentic fit for you is likely your best way to improve your life and, subsequently, help improve the lives of your family, your friends, the members of your community, and ultimately the entire world. Your work may be building quality houses, being an excellent physician, teaching with passion, running a business with integrity, or being an exemplary employee. Find the work that releases your strongest talents and passions, and you will join the growing ranks of those who experience *No More Dreaded Mondays*.

How to Change the World

Here's a good starting point for making the world a better place. This is an inscription written on a tomb dated A.D. 1100 of an Anglican bishop in the crypts of Westminster Abbey:

> *When I was young and free and my imagination had no limits,*
> *I dreamed of changing the world.*
> *As I grew older and wiser I discovered the world would not change—*
> *So I shortened my sights somewhat and decided to change only my country,*
> *But it too seemed immovable.*
> *As I grew into my twilight years, in one last desperate attempt,*
> *I settled for changing only my family, those closest to me,*
> *But alas, they would have none of it.*
> *And now I realize as I lie on my deathbed, if I had only changed myself first,*
> *Then by example I might have changed my family,*
> *From their inspiration and encouragement I would then have been able to better my country,*
> *And who knows, I might have even changed the world.*

NO MORE DREADED MONDAYS
RESOURCES

The Internet provides a wealth of useful information. However, it is also a living, changing resource, providing deception as well as valuable resources that come and go on a daily basis. Learn to use it with discretion. Double-check any information against other sources. Know that as of this writing, the following Internet links provided the information we consider useful.

For a free updated electronic copy of this appendix with live hyperlinks for easy browsing, go to http://48daysblog.wordpress.com/no-more-mondays-appendix/.

Want to Work from Home?

Yes, it really is possible to work from home. As more of you are looking for creative ways to control your time but still create significant income, you will want to be aware of new kinds of opportunities.

Having a thirty-second commute is very appealing. I've enjoyed that for years, not wasting time on traveling, fighting traffic, or hanging around the watercooler discussing last night's sitcoms. It's easy to start a long list of benefits of working from home:

- No nasty commute

- Safety at home rather than risk in a high-rise office building
- Six more weeks a year
- Fancy wardrobe optional
- Lunch from the fridge rather than at expensive restaurants
- Flexible work hours
- (Add your own here)

But Is It Legal?

There are some legitimate questions to be asked about working from home. But most are easily addressed. Working from home does not need to be a complex challenge.

- Check your city's zoning ordinances regarding working from home.
- Check your property's zoning.
  a. Restrictions regarding traffic
  b. Restrictions regarding noise
  c. Outside signs
  d. On-street parking
  e. Employees
  f. Customers—retail selling
  g. Storage of materials
- Keep good relationships with your neighbors.
- Use a PO box or office suite as your business mailing address.
- Apply for a use permit—or variance.

Interested in Telecommuting?

You will find opportunities for artists, desktop publishers, photographers, salespeople, writers, engineers, programmers, data entry clerks, and many others. Check out http://www.jobstele

commuting.com for hundreds of telecommuting jobs. And here are other sites of interest:

http://www.work-at-home-businesses.com

http://www.workathome-businesses.com

http://www.work-home-job-opportunity.com

(Note: Some of these sites will charge for information. Use discretion. As with any opportunity, check out each possibility thoroughly.)

Some of the Best Jobs for Telecommuting

Accountant, auditor, bookkeeper, budget analyst, abstractor, columnist, copywriter, editor, reporter, researcher, technical writer, transcriber, translator, word processor, computer service technician, data entry clerk, database administrator, graphic artist, information specialist, LAN manager, medical records technician, programmer, records manager, systems analyst, Web designer and other Internet-related professional, fund-raiser, real estate agent, sales representative, telemarketer, architect, customer service representative, human resources consultant, lawyer, market researcher, probation officer, public relations specialist, and travel agent.

You may be surprised to learn that it's possible to transition from your current position into telework. Here's a great overview of how to make your case for telecommuting: http://www.quint careers.com/telecommuting_options.html.

What would your company like to save money on?
- Rent
- Utilities
- Parking
- Wardrobe

"You" for Sale

For decades, companies have been using the same methods for finding workers: newspaper ads, word of mouth, family connections, and recruiters. An interesting development is occurring now with the ease of using the Internet. More and more companies are putting out projects and allowing people to bid on them.

Talented Revolutionary workers are also putting their skills up for bid. At www.elanceonline.com you can find projects available in sales, writing, management, administration, architecture, law, and more. At http://www.gofreelance.com there are even more opportunities in writing, editing, graphic design, and programming. If you have skills in any area, you can list your availability and go to the highest bidder. Nurses will find opportunities at www.travelnursedepot.com. There are new opportunities appearing every day.

As always in a healthy work economy, you must be very clear about your marketable skills. Once you have identified your strongest areas of competence, the options for generating revenue become very interesting.

Interested in Unusual Work?

Here are a few great resources:

- Moms to Work kit: http://www.jobsandmoms.com/Back-to-Work-Toolkit.htm
- Moms working from home: http://webmomz.com/index.shtml
- The Employment Guide's listing of work-at-home opportunities: http://www.employmentguide.com/All_Work_At_Home_Jobs/ALL/workathomesearch_results.html

Thinking about Consulting?

Here are a few consulting associations you should check out:

- Association of Professional Consultants: http://www
.consultapc.org
- Institute of Management Consultants USA: http://www
.imcusa.org
- Association of Management Consulting Firms (features the
leading associations of consultants and firms around the world):
http://www.amcf.org/index.asp
- You can go here to create a personalized independent contractor's agreement ($15): http://jobsearchtech.about.com/od/
jobs/l/aa083099_4.htm

Launching a Business? What's Your Plan?

If you are doing something small on your own, I can give you a
simple Business Planning Guide to get you started: http://48days
.faithsite.com/content.asp?CID=14694.

If you are going to borrow money, raise venture capital, have
lots of employees, and own real estate, you will need a more
comprehensive business plan. Here are a few sites to get you
started:

http://www.entrepreneur.com/businessplan/index.html
http://www.inc.com/guides/start_biz/20660.html
http://www.bplans.com
http://www.sba.gov/starting_business/planning/basic.html
http://www.nolo.com/resource.cfm/catID/E67C08E9-9F
AE-4AD8=840371947878E573/111/228/289/

Luck is what happens to people who have clear goals and detailed plans of action.

Legal Information You Need to Know

Research what you will need to know about federal, state, and local licenses and taxes. Every state has an Internet site where you can quickly and easily access forms, licenses, et cetera. You can find your state by Googling "Ohio government," or whatever. When it comes to a business license start-up or working from home, my philosophy is "Keep it simple." Don't make things more complicated than they need to be.

Whether you're going to launch an eBay business or a window-washing service or start selling home-baked cheesecakes, you can do those things without any complex process. You can simply show it as miscellaneous income on your income taxes. There is nothing misrepresentative about that when you're just starting your venture. Just make sure it's declared as part of your income tax return.

Business licenses typically cost about twenty dollars a year. If you get one of those, it will start the ball rolling on some other processes. You will be asked to submit year-end records. In most counties in the United States, there'll be some small percentage occupational tax. There may be a franchise and excise tax depending on how you're structured.

You don't need to do anything complicated in terms of forming a corporation or a limited liability company unless you really are going to start a large-scale business. My philosophy is to start small. When you see that you're going to generate fifty to sixty thousand dollars a year, you might want to look at the possibility of forming an LLC or an S corporation, which are the most likely appropriate corporate structures for the kinds of businesses we're talking about.

You do need a sales-and-use tax license if you're going to buy things at wholesale and resell them—even products that are components of something else you're going to sell. For example, if you want to buy ingredients for the brownies you make without having to pay tax, you get a resale license. Then you collect tax on the product you sell.

• You'll find lots of free downloadable business forms here: http://www.legalbusinessforms.com
• Here you can get your forms specific to your state. Not free, but well worth it: http://partners.uslegalforms.com/enter.php?a=48days

Distinguishing Between Self-Employed Individuals and Independent Contractors

You are self-employed if any of the following apply to you:

• You carry on a trade or business as a sole proprietor.
• You are a member of a partnership or limited liability company that files a Form 1065, U.S. Return of Partnership Income, and carries on a trade or business.
• You are otherwise in business for yourself.

You are also self-employed if you have a part-time business in addition to your regular job.

Still have questions? This site can help: http://www.irs.gov/businesses/small/article/0,,id=115041,00.html.

Free Ideas!

One of the most popular methods today for structuring any business option is implementing it as a home-based business idea. More possibilities pop up daily. The best way for me to keep sharing new ideas is through my free weekly newsletter, which you can find at http://www.48Days.com.

In addition to most franchises, business opportunities, and distributorships being practiced as home-based businesses, here are some more ideas to stimulate your thinking:

Accounting services
Aerial photography
Animal training
Apartment finding
Appliance repair
Auto detailing
Balloon vending
Bed-and-breakfast hosting
Bicycle repair
Business consulting
Cake decorating
Career coaching
Catering
Ceiling fan installation
Child security systems
    installation
Child transportation
Chimney cleaning
Computer services
Consignment sales
Custom-made candy
    making
Deck and covering
    installation
Delivery service
Electroplating
Event planning
Flea market vending

Gift basket creation
Graphic design
Home inspection
Home schooling
    counseling
Hospital flower vending
Hot dog sales
Housecleaning
House painting
Import/export brokerage
    service
Independent sales agent
Interior decorating
Internet marketing
Jewelry sales
Kitchen renovation
Landscaping
Lawn service
Leading training seminars
Mail-order business
Manners instruction
Mobile car washing
Newsletter publication
Nutrition counseling
Organic gardening
Pet sitting
Printer-cartridge recharging
Portrait painting

Power washing

Public relations and marketing

Real estate photography

Roofing

Selling discount coupon books

Senior citizen care

Sewing alterations

Tree removal

Tutoring

Used stereo equipment sales

Website design

Wedding photography

Wedding planning

Window display design

Window tinting

Writing how-to books

Add your own ideas:

_____

_____

_____

_____

_____

Look through the backs of all those newsstand magazines. Yes, there is plenty of garbage there, but you find the great options by getting familiar with a lot of them. Send for information from twenty to thirty companies, and you'll begin to see what makes sense.

> *If we listened to our intellect, we'd never have a love affair. We'd never have a friendship. We'd never go into business, because we'd be cynical. Well, that's nonsense. You've got to jump off the cliff all the time and build your wings on the way down.*
>
> —Ray Bradbury

Helpful Internet Sites
For Those Interested in Revolutionary Work

http://www.workingsolo.com
This site lists twelve hundred business resources for those seeking self-employment.

http://www.sbaonline.sba.gov
This is the U.S. Small Business Administration site, which provides a massive amount of information and links.

http://www.nfibonline.com
A wonderful site by the National Federation of Independent Business, giving daily information concerning legislation affecting small business and a great variety of tips for being successful.

http://www.entrepreneurmag.com/magazine
This site lists businesses for sale, business building information, business opportunities, and much more.

http://www.homebusiness.com
Home Business Solutions

http://www.timknox.com/resources.php
Small Business Resources—articles, database of franchise and business opportunities

http://www.hoaa.com
Home Office Association of America

http://www.nationalbusiness.org
National Business Association

http://www.nmbc.org
The National Minority Business Council

http://www.soho.org
SOHO is Small Office Home Office. This site offers help for the challenges of working in a small office/home office environment.

http://www.gmarketing.com
The complete Guerilla Marketing site offers books, resources, chat rooms, and updates on issues affecting your business.

http://www.disgruntled.com
This really is a site for unhappy people to tell their work stories. Last year over 800,000 people lost their jobs, and millions more are just not happy.

http://www.franchise.org
The International Franchise Association is the membership organization of franchisers, franchisees, and suppliers.

http://www.aaede.org
Asian American Economic Development Enterprises Inc. helps create business and personal growth for Asian Americans and others through education, employment, and enterprise.

http://www.asianbiz.com
The Asian Business Association helps Asian American business owners gain access to economic opportunities.

http://www.nhba.org
The National Hispanic Business Association promotes the advancement and training of Hispanic businesses.

http://www.nase.org
The National Association for the Self-Employed assists small business owners with the services, resources, and benefits of large companies.

http://www.nawbo.org
The National Association of Women Business Owners represents the interests of female entrepreneurs.

http://www.sbsc.org
The Small Business Entrepreneurship Council is an advocacy group for small business.

http://www.wcoeusa.org
Women Construction Owners and Executives, USA, promotes members through marketing, financing, and legislative action.

http://www.uschamber.org
The U.S. Chamber of Commerce offers much information about all business questions.

http://www.anderson.ucla.edu/research/esc/welcome.htm
The UCLA Harold and Pauline Price Center for Entrepreneurial Studies provides a set of academic and extracurricular experiences that advance the theory and practice of entrepreneurship.

http://www.wboc.org
The Women Business Owners Corporation offers national certification for women-owned companies.

http://www.uspto.gov
The U.S. Patent and Trademark Office. All patent information, including attorneys and agents. Forms can be printed.

http://www.workingfromhome.com
http://www.paulandsarah.com
Paul and Sarah Edwards's site gives self-employment tips.

http://www.myboss.com
This resource site has links to other sites offering information on work-from-home options, home-based businesses, background checks on employees, and much more.

http://www.business.gov
This U.S. government site can help you identify and comply with federal regulations and links you to the Internal Revenue Service, the Social Security Administration, the Occupational Safety and Health Administration, and numerous other federal agencies. You can also obtain federal tax information by calling the IRS at 800-TAX-FORM.

http://www.apple.com
http://www.compusa.com
http://www.compaq.com
http://www.dell.com
http://www.gateway.com
These secure shopping sites feature both low-cost and high-end business computers.

http://www.smallbizsearch.com
This massive site allows you to search the world of small business from one place on the Internet. It will provide fast, accurate results to nearly all your questions.

http://www.smallbizbooks.com
This site offers a secure online shopping environment where you can peruse or purchase entrepreneurs' business start-up guides.

You'll find lots of tools to help you plan, run, and grow your business.

http://www.cnbc.com/id/15838512
The Big Idea: Donny Deutsch. The website for this weekly show on CNBC profiles ideas that have been turned into million-dollar businesses.

NOTES

2. Let Your Life Speak

1. Stephen R. Covey, *First Things First* (New York: Simon & Schuster, 1994), p. 45.

2. Dan Miller, *48 Days to the Work You Love: An Interactive Study* (Nashville: Broadman & Holman, 2005), p. 47.

3. Rumi, "Forget Your Life," in *The Enlightened Heart*, ed. Stephen Mitchell (New York: HarperCollins, 1989), p. 56.

4. Thomas Merton, "Hagia Sophia," in *A Thomas Merton Reader*, ed. Thomas P. McConnell (New York: Doubleday, 1989), p. 506.

5. Harison Wein, "Stress and Disease: New Perspectives," http://www.nih.gov/news/WordonHealth/oct2000/story01.htm (last accessed April 12, 2007).

6. *The Inferno of Dante: A New Verse Translation*, trans. Robert Pinsky (New York: Noonday Press, 1994), 1:1–7.

3. Who's Making Your Lunch Today?

1. Craig Boldman and Pete Matthews, *Every Excuse in the Book* (Kansas City, Mo.: Andrews McMeel), pp. 3–8.

4. Don't Wait for the "Wizard"

1. Thomas Stanley, *The Millionaire Mind* (Kansas City, Mo.: Andrews McMeel, 2000), p. 161.

2. Home of America's Hot Dog King, http://www.allamericanhot dog.com.

5. Donald's Not Coming — Fire Yourself!

1. Daniel Goleman, Paul Kaufman, and Michael Ray, *The Creative Mind* (New York: Plume, 1993), p. 31.

2. Bob Rosner, Working Wounded Blog, http://www.abcnews.go.com/Business/WorkingWounded/story?id=622793 (last accessed May 9, 2006).

3. http://biz.yahoo.com/special/allbiz120606_article1.html (last accessed April 26, 2007).

4. R. G. H. Siu, *The Craft of Power* (Melbourne, FL: Krieger Publishing, 1985).

5. U.S. Department of Labor, "Fastest Growing Occupations," http://www.bls.gov/emp/emptab21.htm (last accessed May 9, 2006).

6. Ibid.

6. "Secure" or "Imprisoned"?

1. Daniel Pink, *Free Agent Nation* (New York: Time Warner, 2001), p. 14.

2. Dolly Parton, *Dolly: My Life and Other Unfinished Business* (New York: HarperCollins Publishers, Inc., 1994), p. 139.

3. http://en.wikipedia.org/wiki/Sunday_Times_Rich_List_2006 (last accessed April 27, 2007).

4. http://en.wikipedia.org/wiki/Walter_Mischel (last accessed April 27, 2007).

5. "The Exceptional Brain of Albert Einstein," http://www.bioquant.com/gallery/einstein.html.

6. Dan Miller, *48 Days to the Work You Love: An Interactive Study* (Nashville: Broadman & Holman, 2005).

7. But You Owe Me

1. http://www.pbs.org/wgbh/aso/databank/entries/dt13as.html (last accessed May 16, 2006).

2. Michael J. Gelb, *How to Think Like Leonardo da Vinci* (New York: Delacorte Press, 1998), p. 158.

8. Finding Work That Fits

1. Scott Adams, *The Dilbert Principle* (New York: Harper Business, 1996), p. 151.

2. http://www.sba.gov/aboutsba/sbastats.html (last accessed May 17, 2006).

3. http://www.bls.gov/bdm/home.htm (last accessed May 17, 2006).

4. Alan Deutschman, *Fast Company* (May 2005), p. 53, http://www.fast company.com/magazine/94/open_change-or-die.html.

5. In Richard Bolles, *The Three Boxes of Life* (Berkeley: Ten Speed Press, 1981), p. 60.

9. One Place Forever—Blessing or Curse?

1. Ross Stokes and Kathy Crockett, "227 Unusual Business Ideas," http://www.unusualbusinessideas.com/cmd.asp?af=395814 (last accessed May 12, 2006).

2. Ibid.

10. Throw Out Your TV (And Your Alarm Clock Too!)

1. Preaching Today, "Upside-Down Christmas Tree," http://preaching today.com/32387 (last accessed May 20, 2006).

2. William H. Danforth, *I Dare You!* (St. Louis: Twenty-Eight Edition, 1980), p. 51.

3. John C. Maxwell, *Developing the Leader Within You* (Nashville: Thomas Nelson, 1993), p. 170.

4. Sarah J. Hale, *Things By Their Right Names, and Other Stories, Fables, and Mural Pieces, in Prose and Verse.* Selected and arranged from the writings of Mrs. Barbauld (Boston: Marsh, Capen, Lyon, and Webb, 1840), p. 29.

11. No Money—No Problem!

1. Yahoo News, http://www.freerepublic.com/focus/f-news/1493068/posts (last accessed May 19, 2006).

2. Brian Tracy, *Getting Rich Your Own Way* (New York: John Wiley, 2004), p. 8.

3. Henry David Thoreau, *Walden*, chap. 1, http://www.transcendental ists.com/walden_economy.htm.

Continue Your
No More Dreaded Mondays
Experience

We invite you to continue your *No More Dreaded Mondays* experience on our Web site, www.NoMoreMondaysBlog.com.

Here are some of the enhanced features you will find:

- Communicate directly with Dan Miller.

- See the new *No More Dreaded Mondays* application guide.

- Share what you're experiencing in your current work.

- Get current updates on the changing face of work.

- Share your insights and discuss the book with other readers.

- See up-to-date opportunities for *No More Dreaded Mondays* work.

- Access free business plan guides to bring your idea to life.

- Join our Coaching network to build your own infopreneuring business.

Come join the *No More Dreaded Mondays* Community

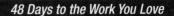

48 DAYS
Coaching Connection